Michael Williams

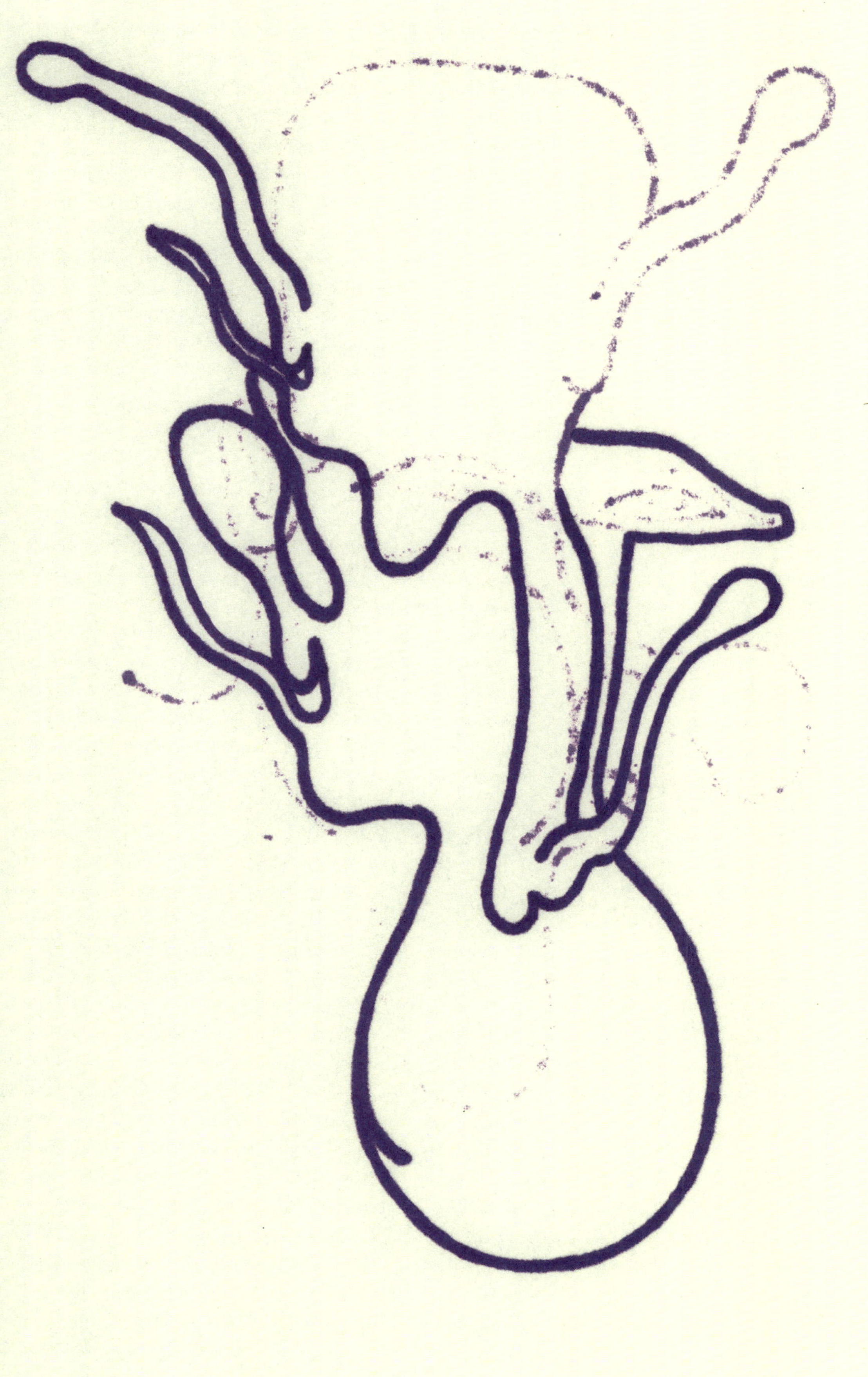

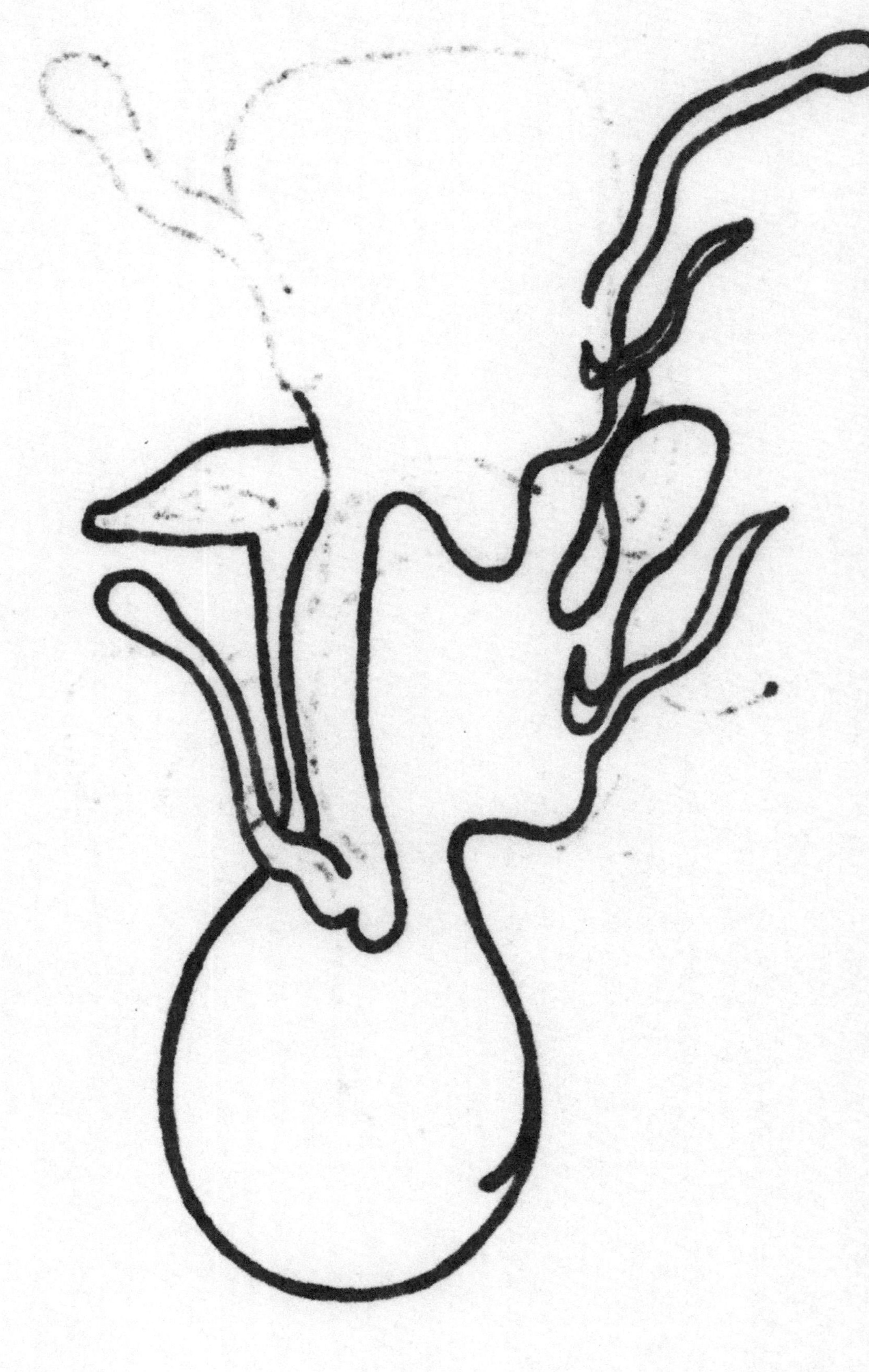

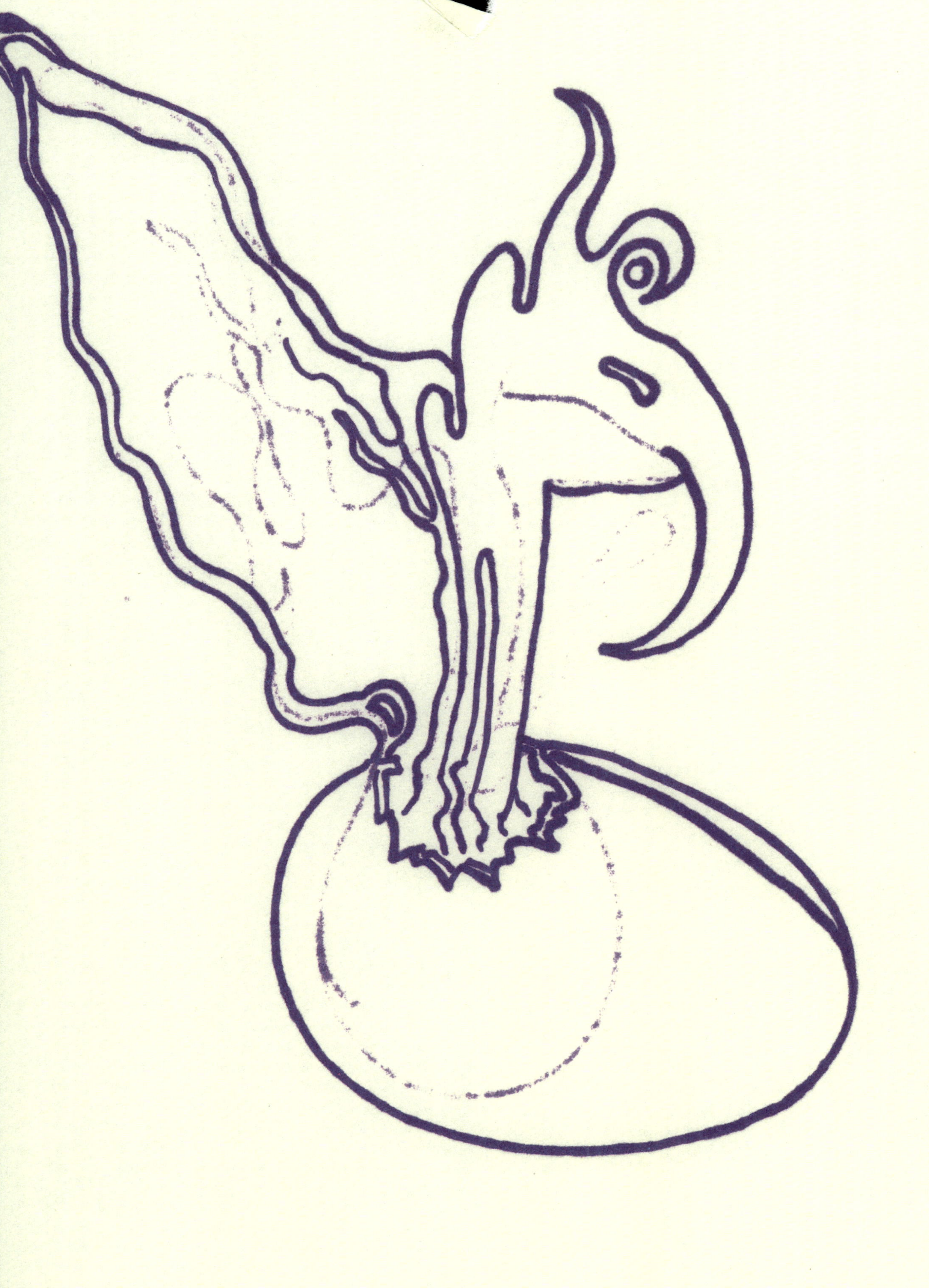

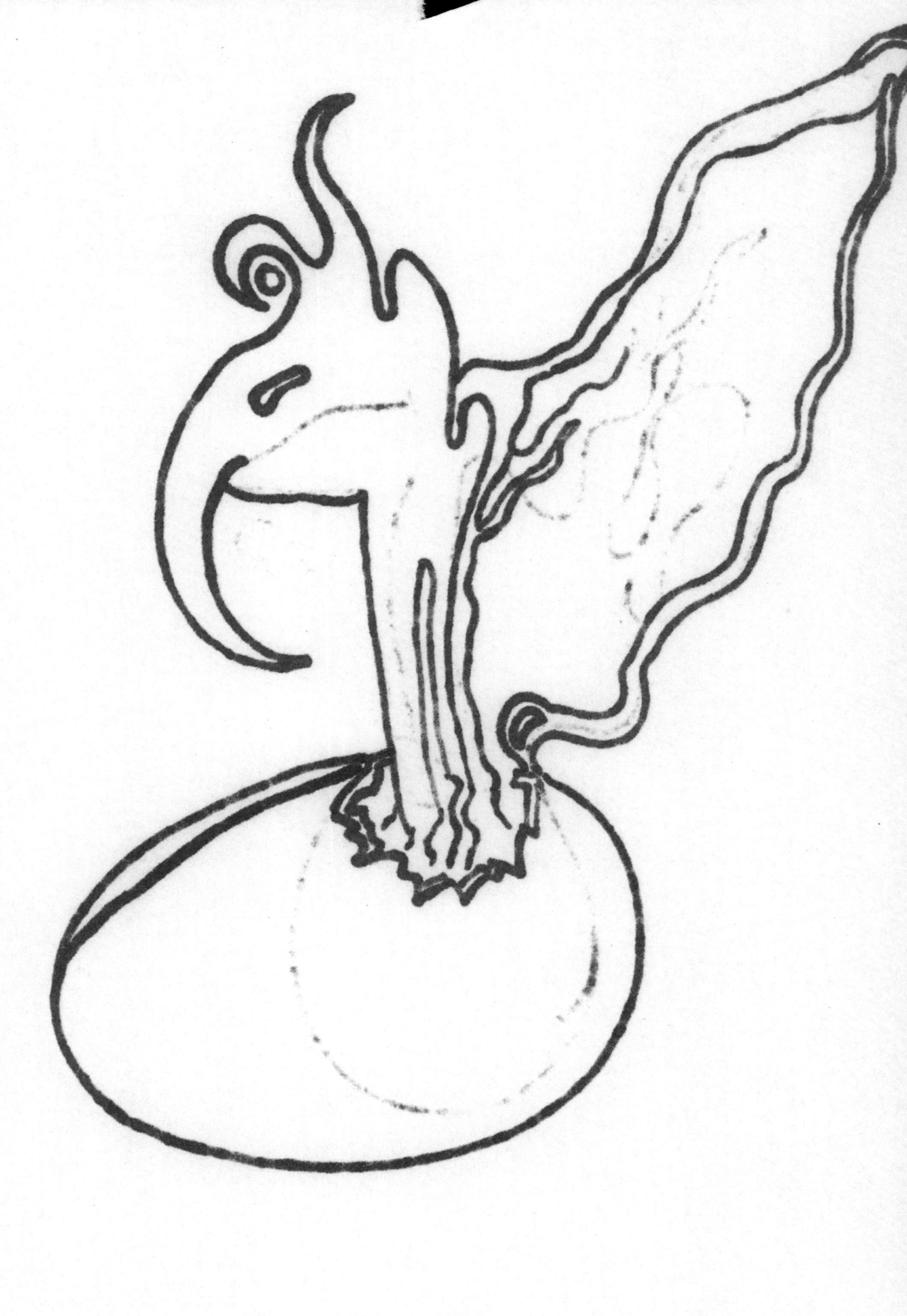

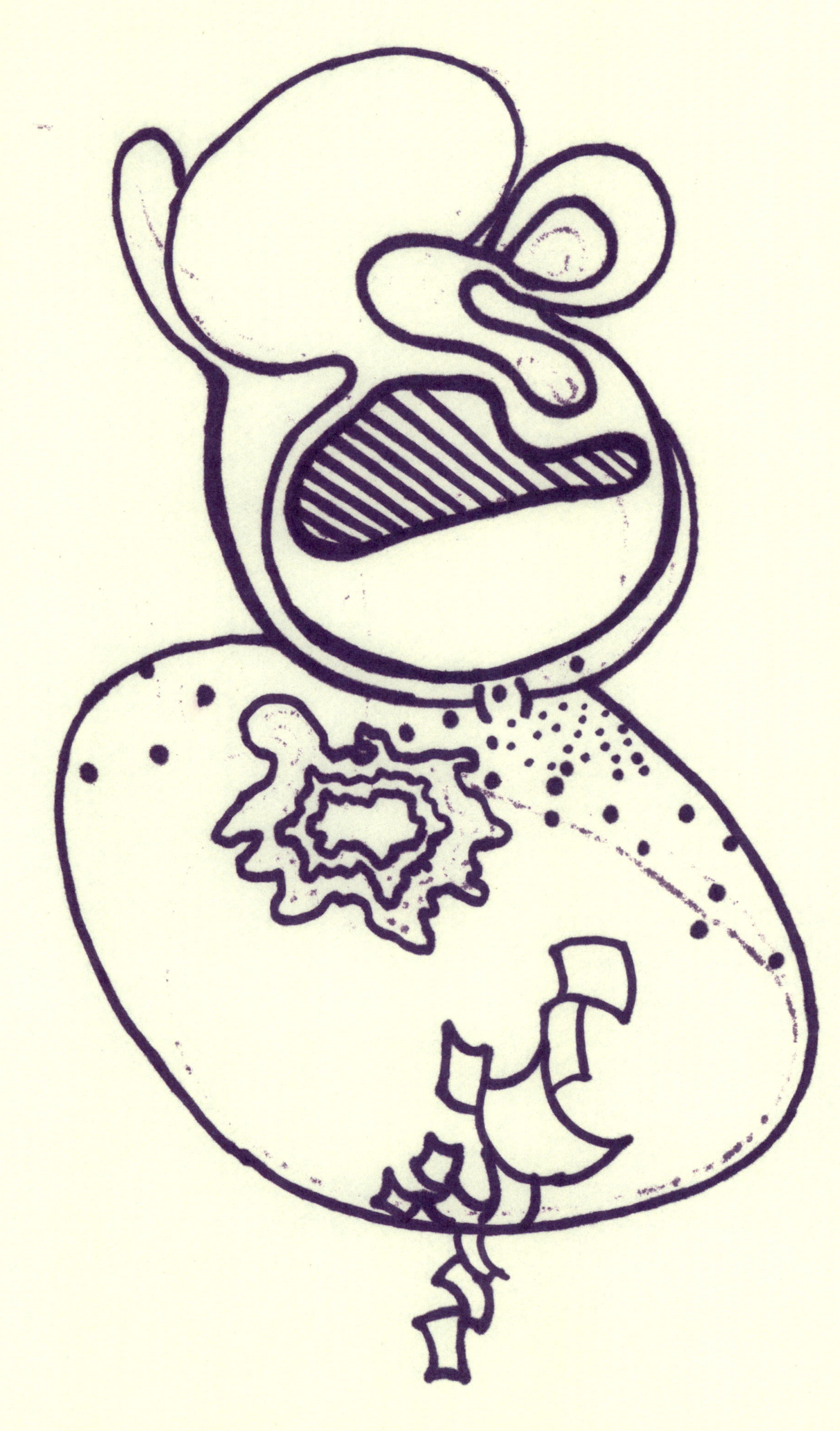

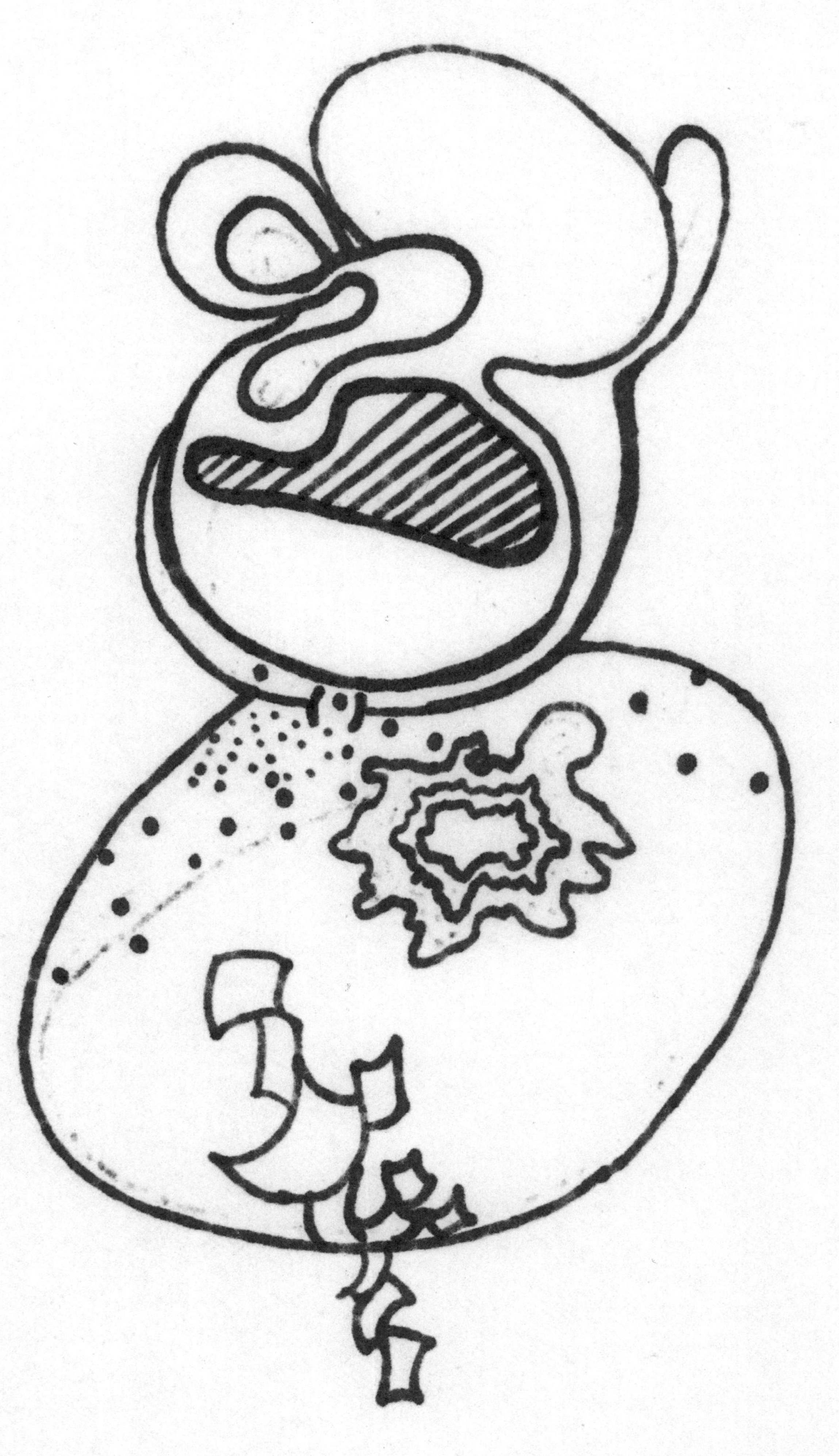

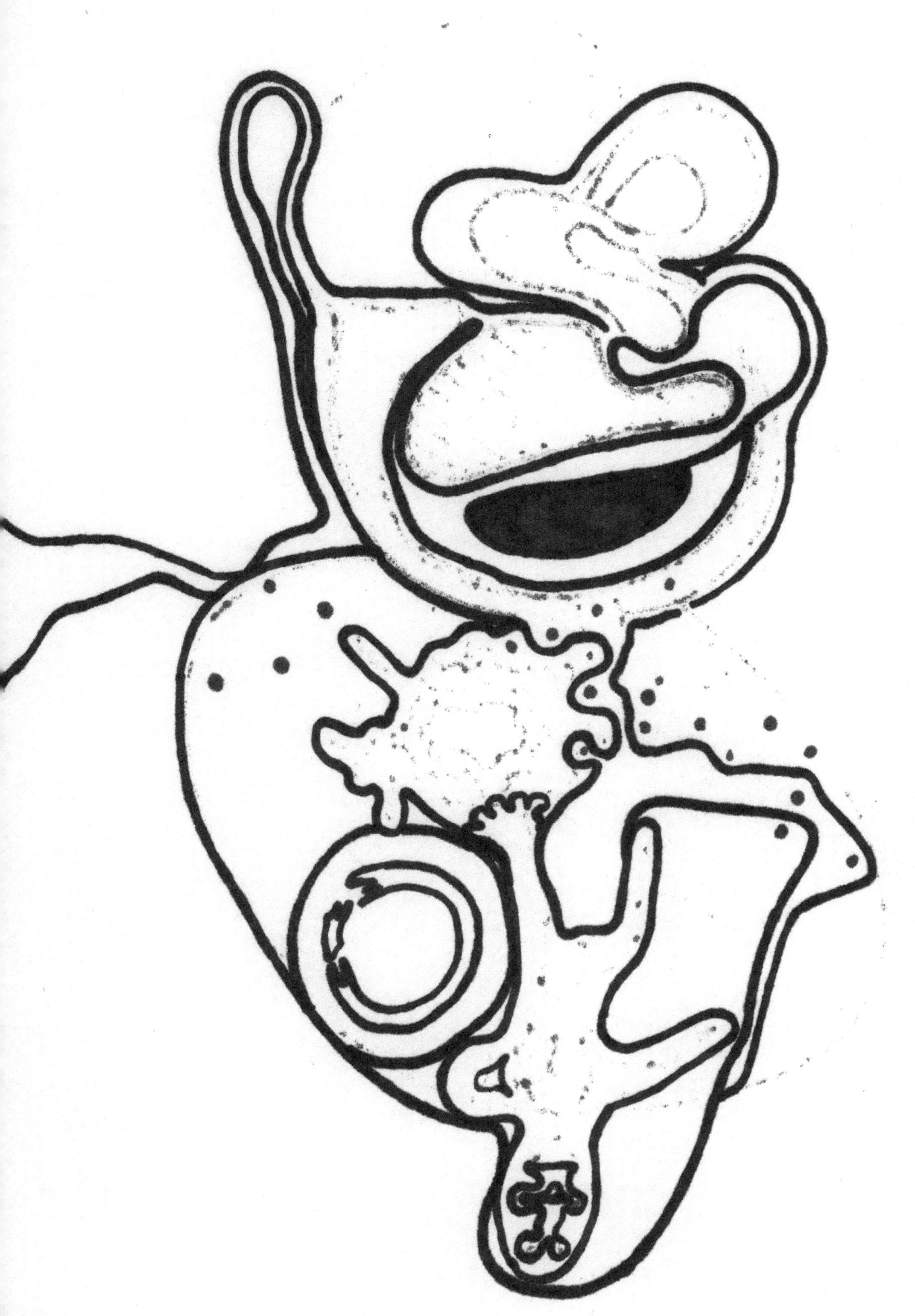

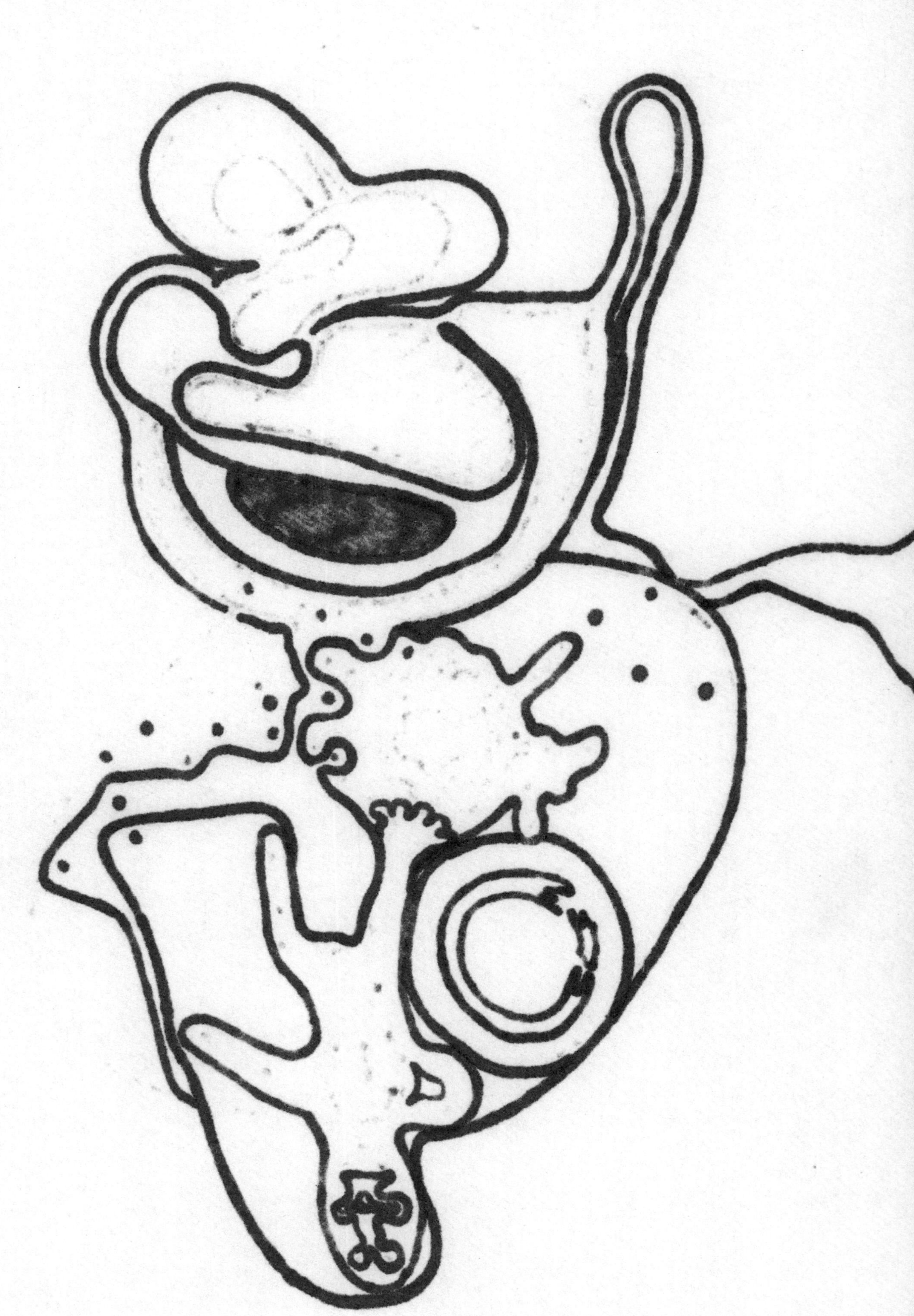

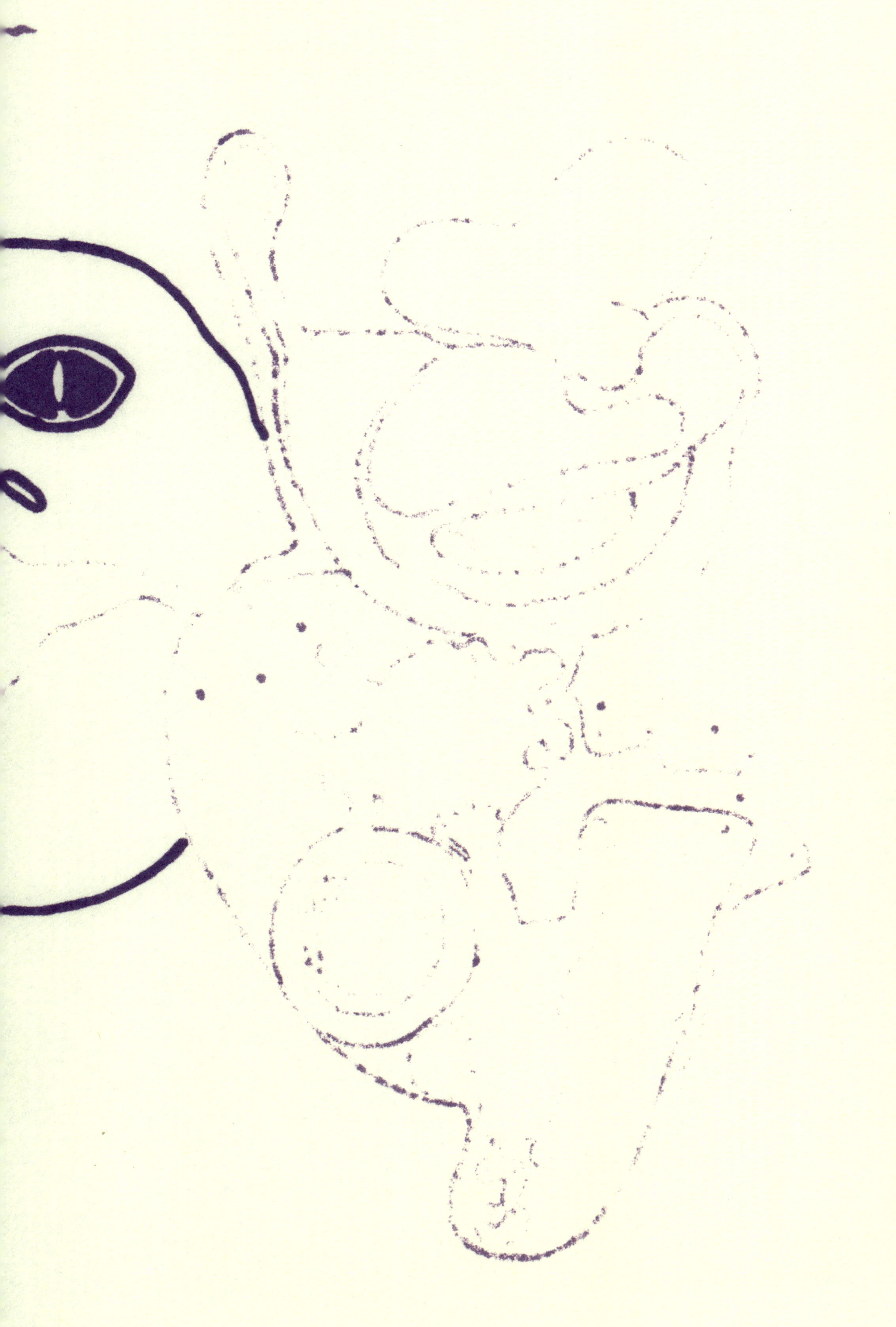

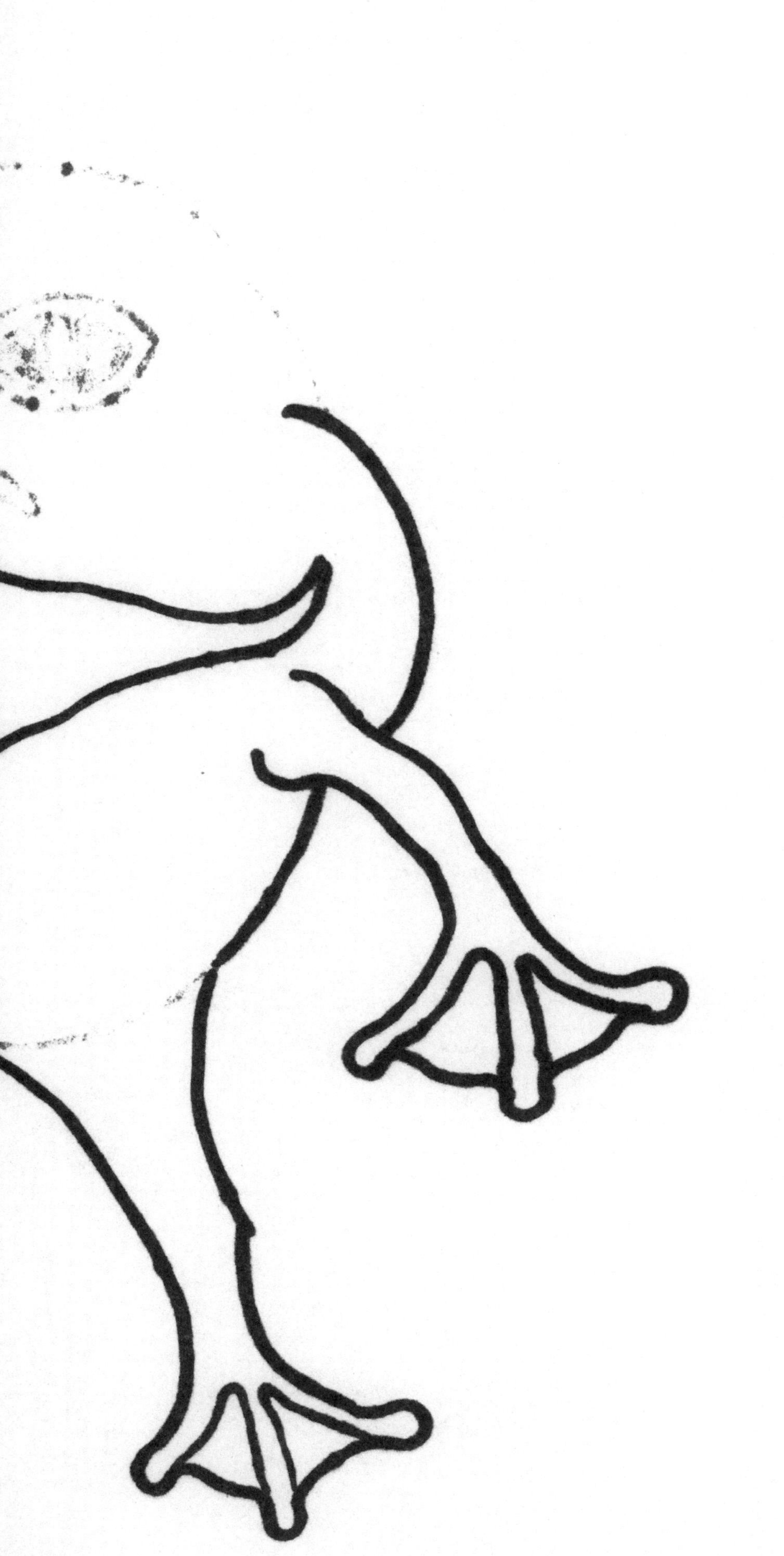

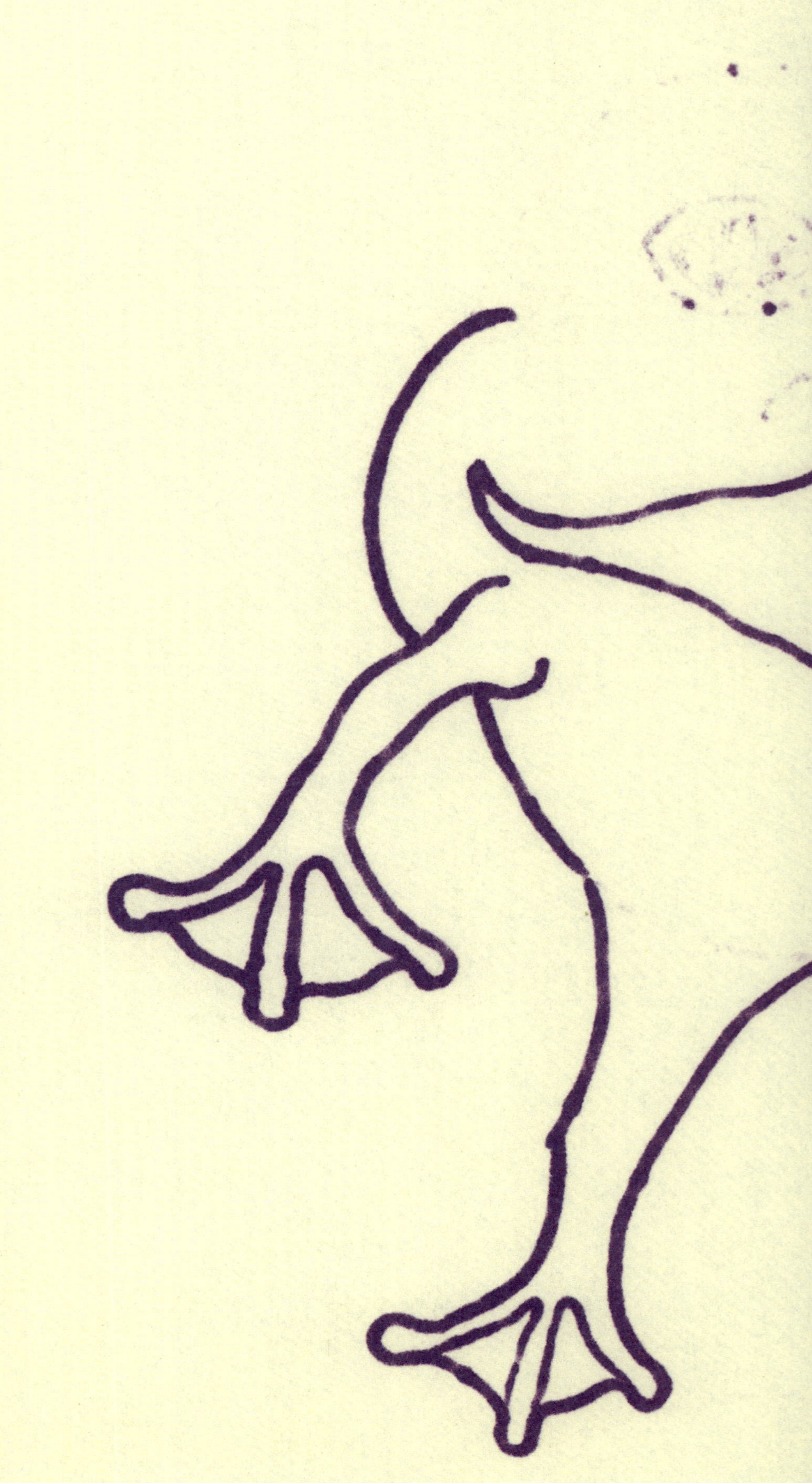

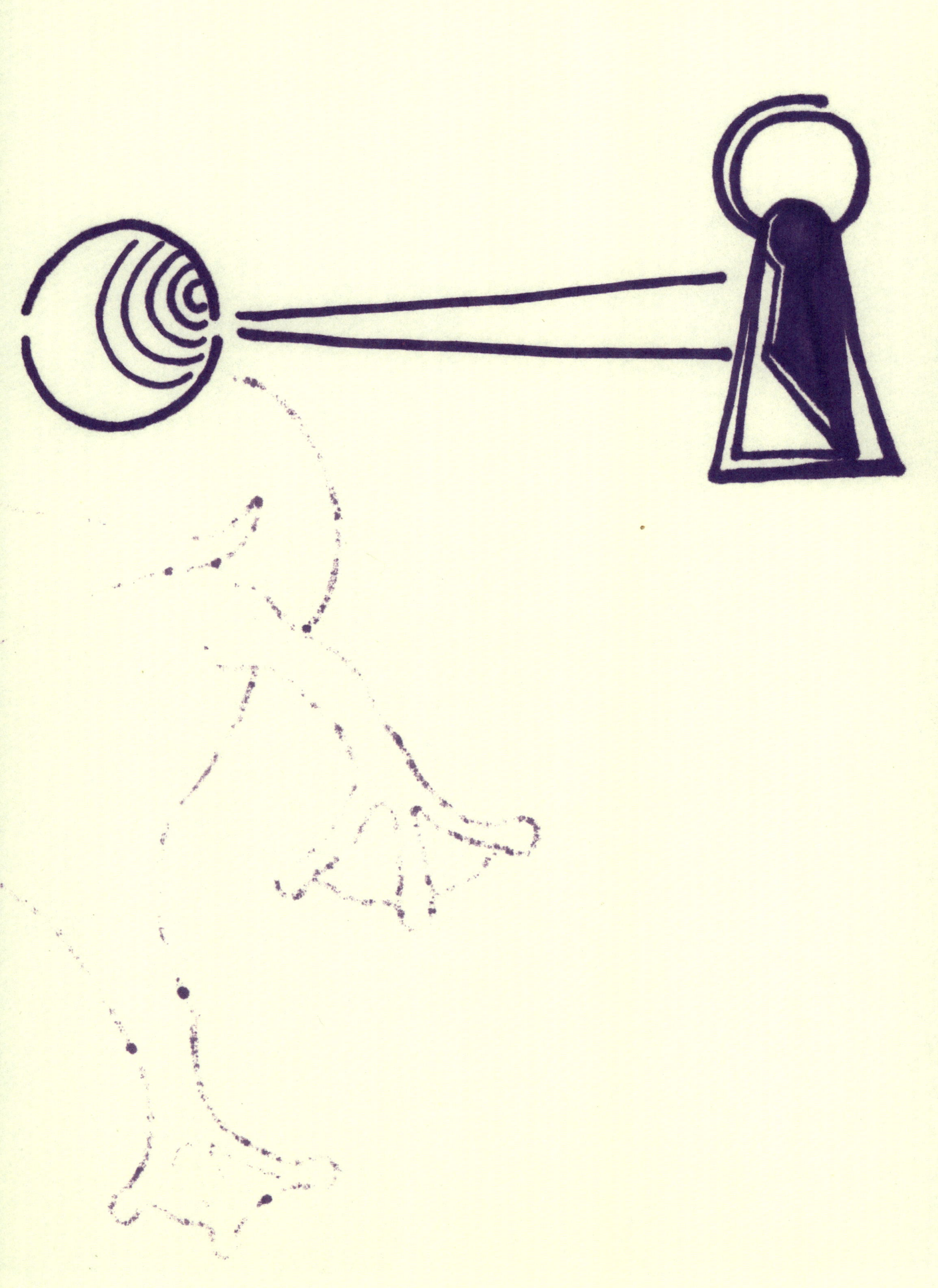

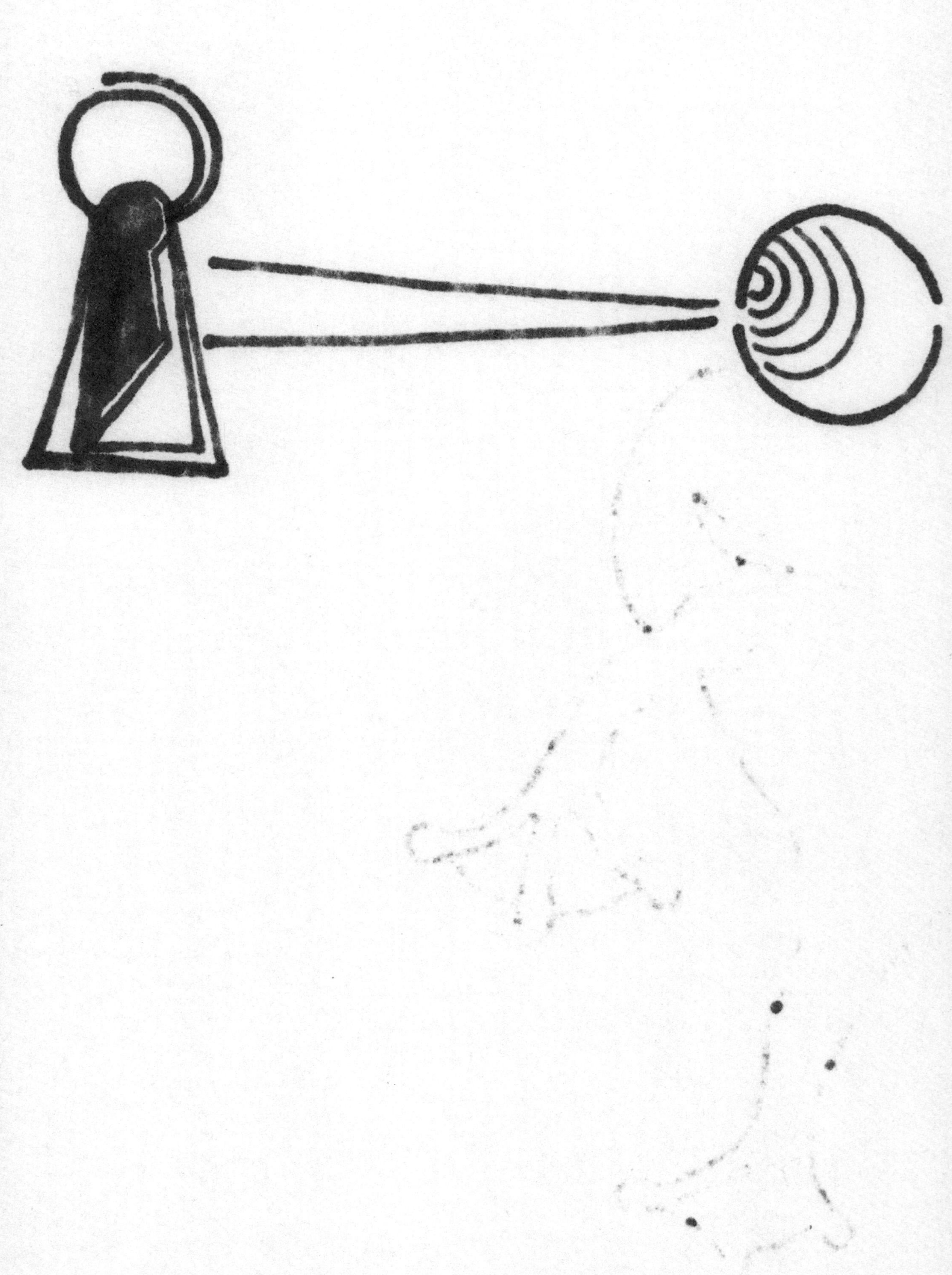

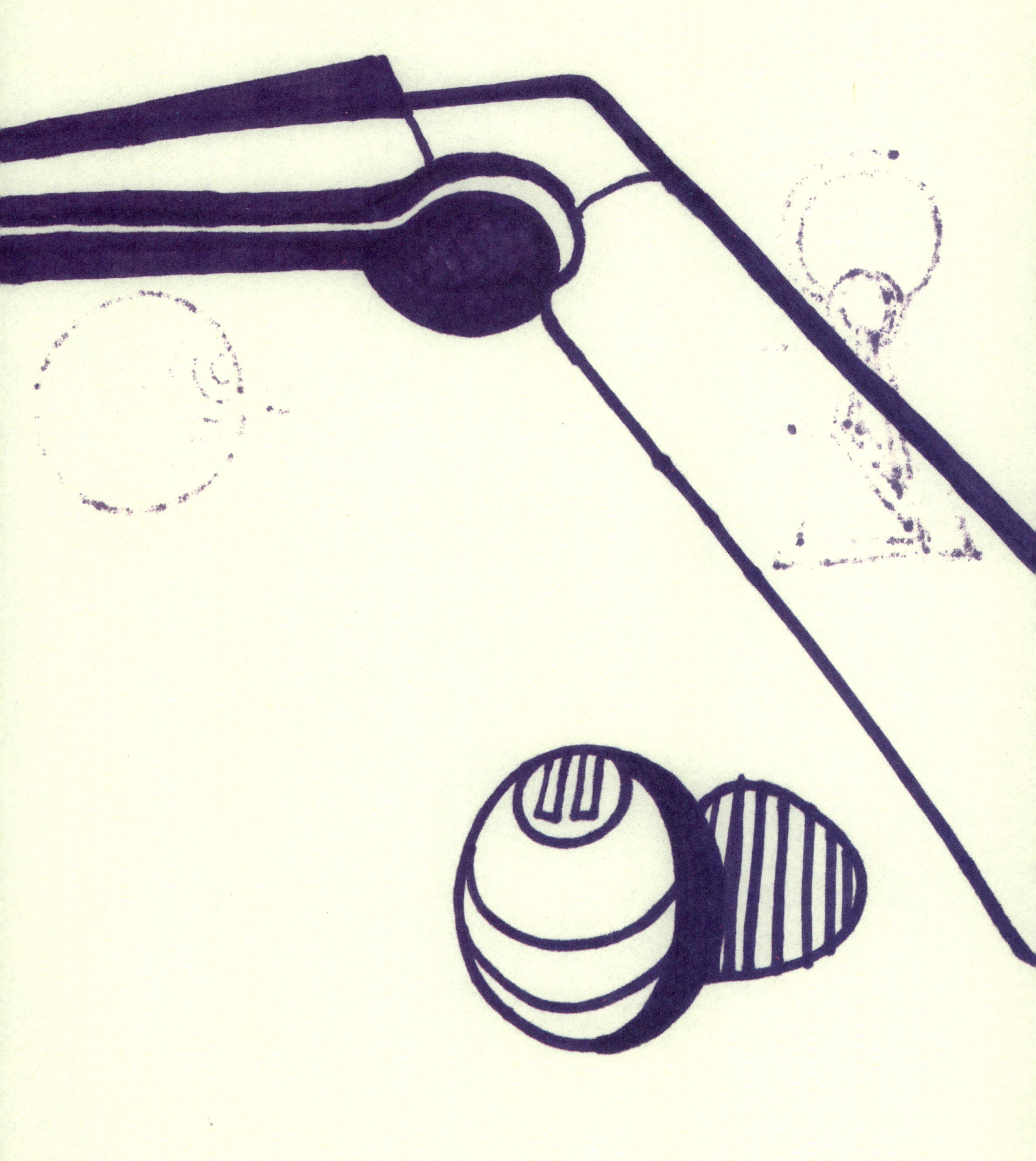

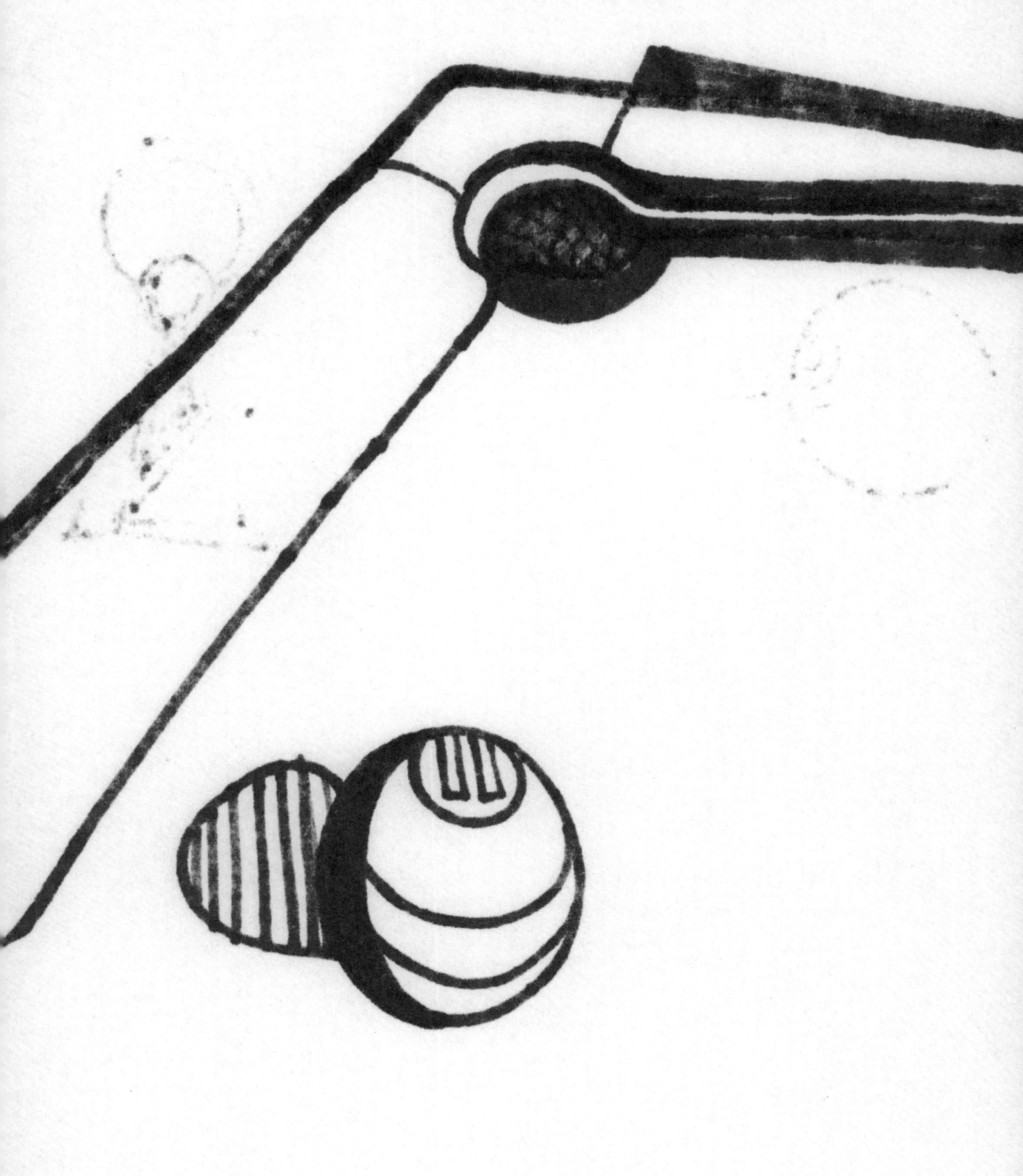

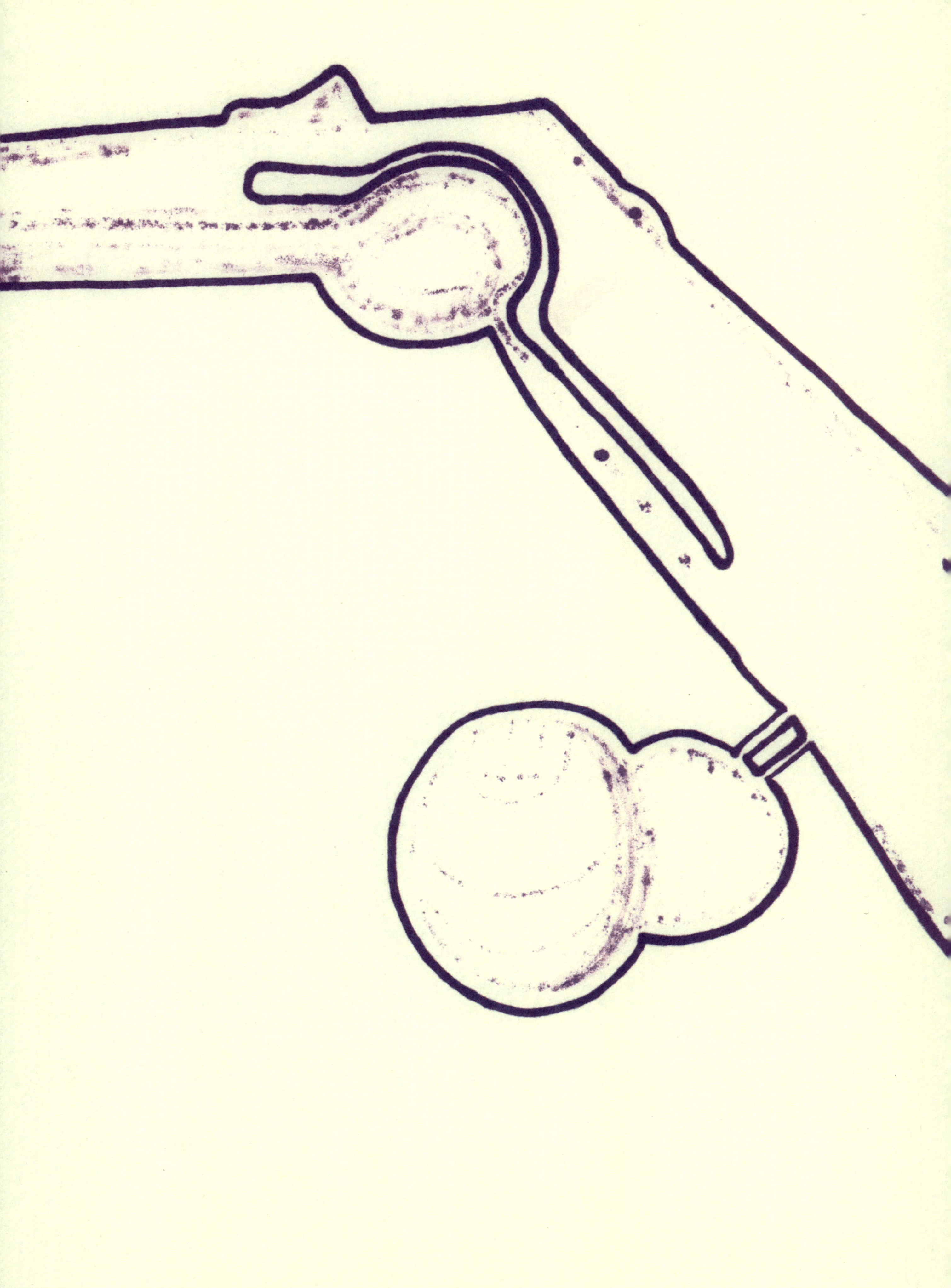

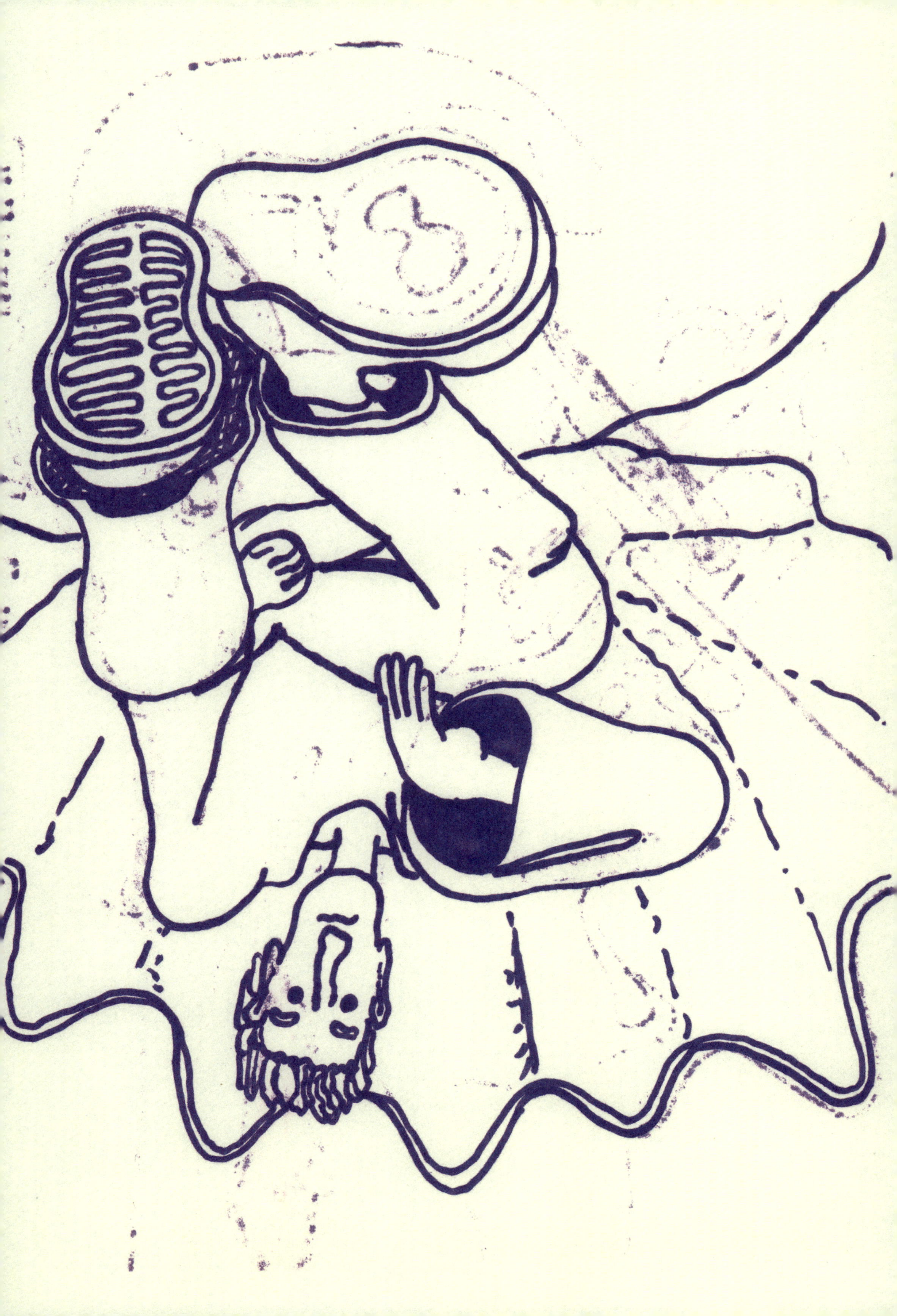

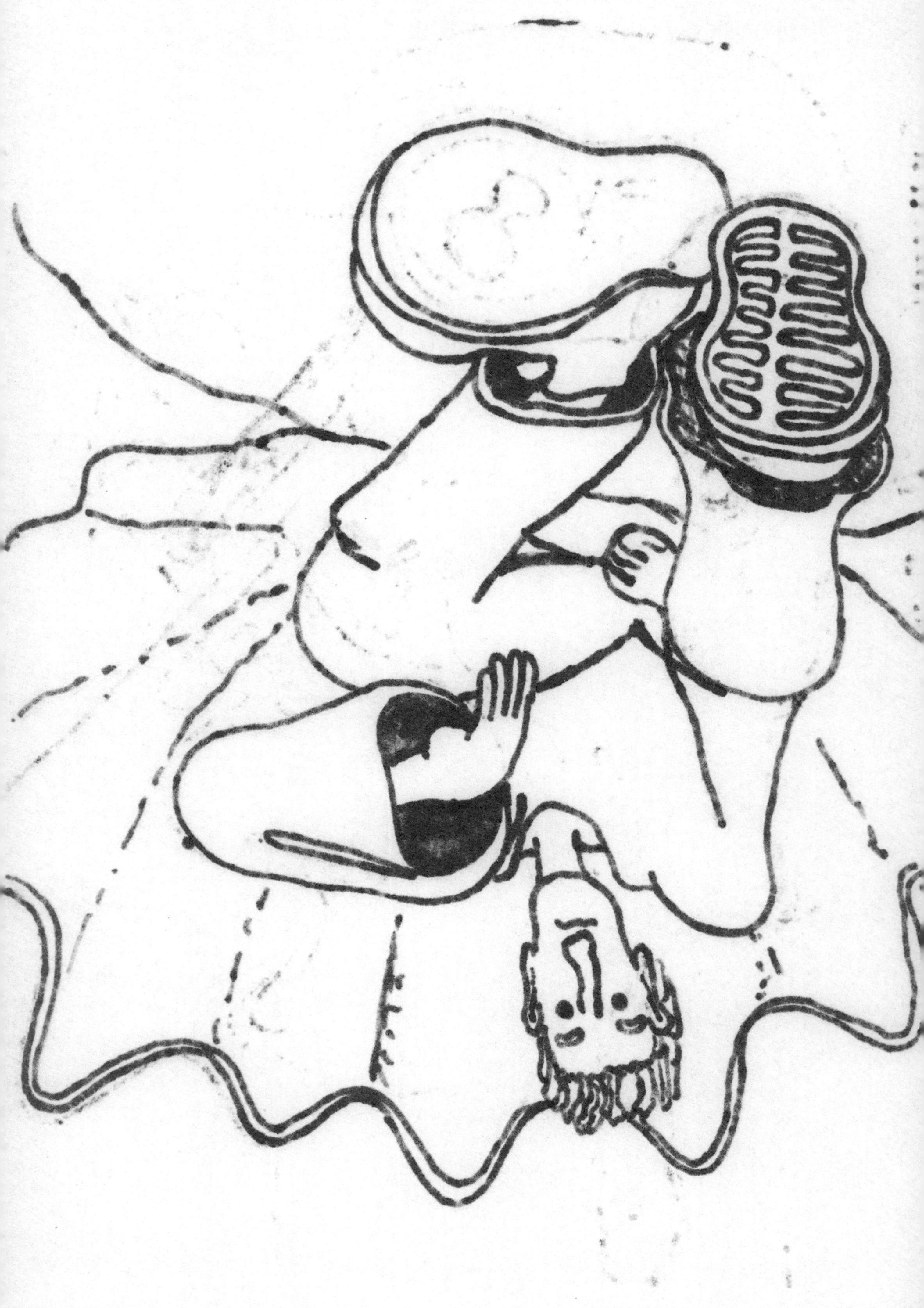

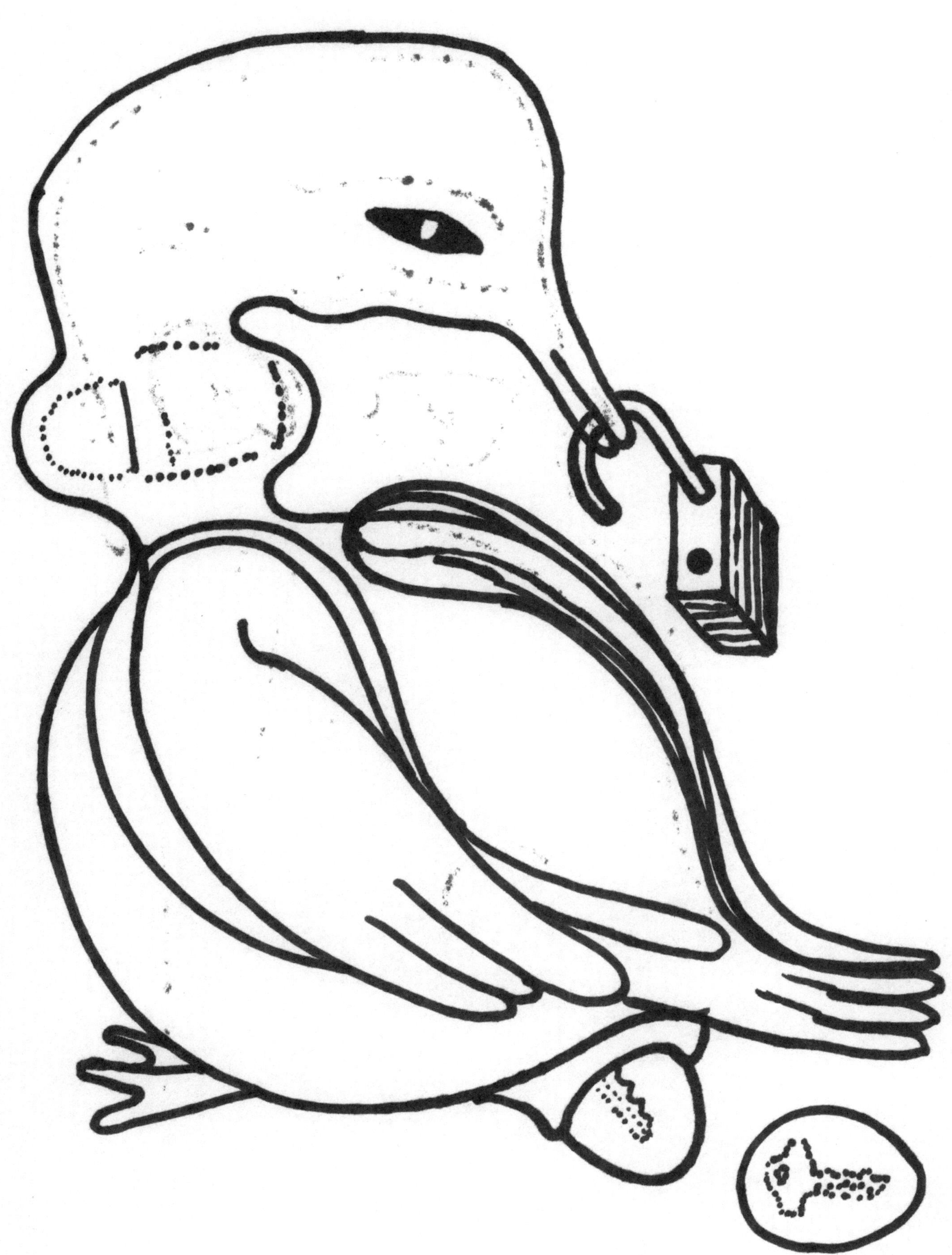

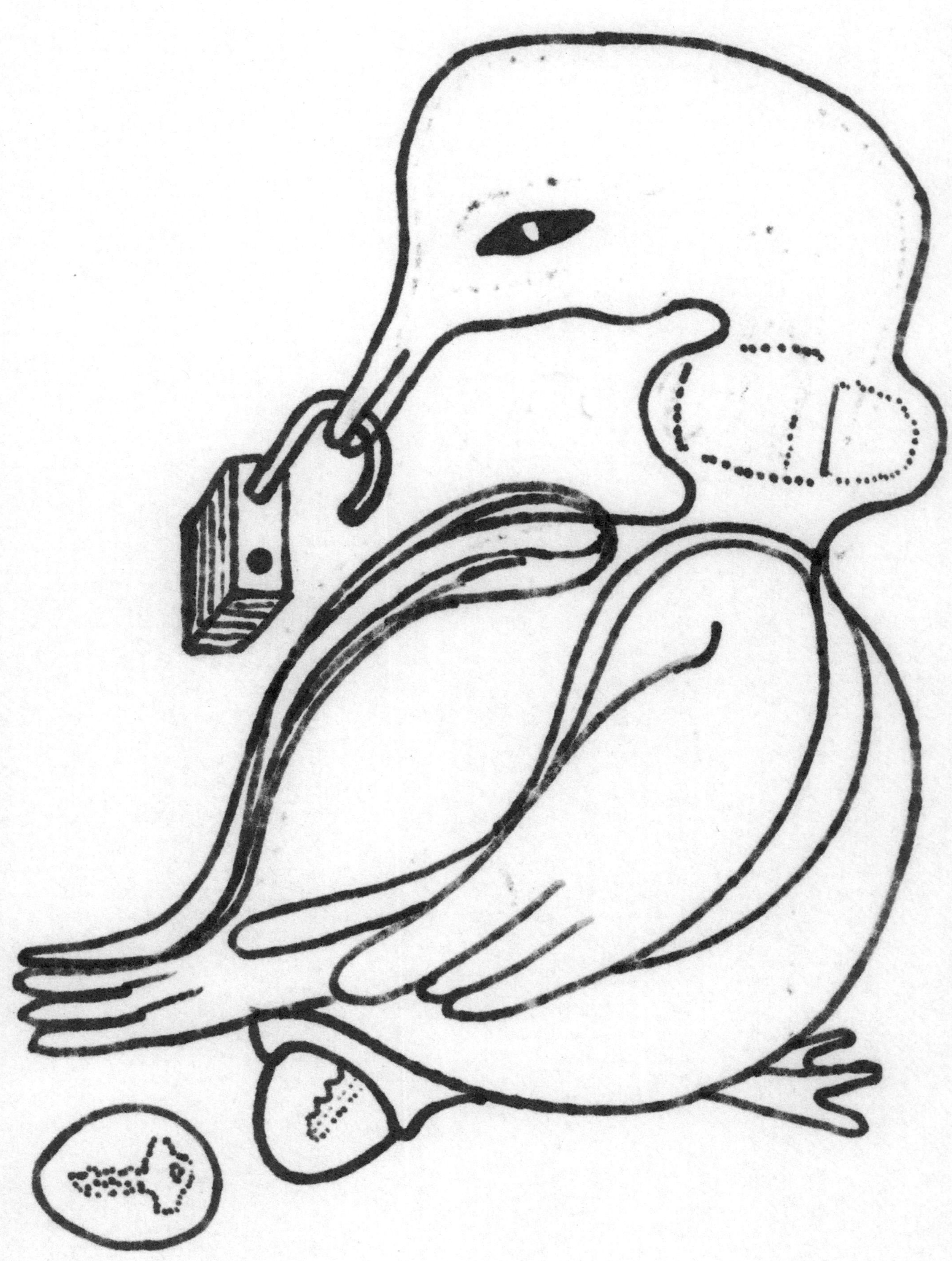

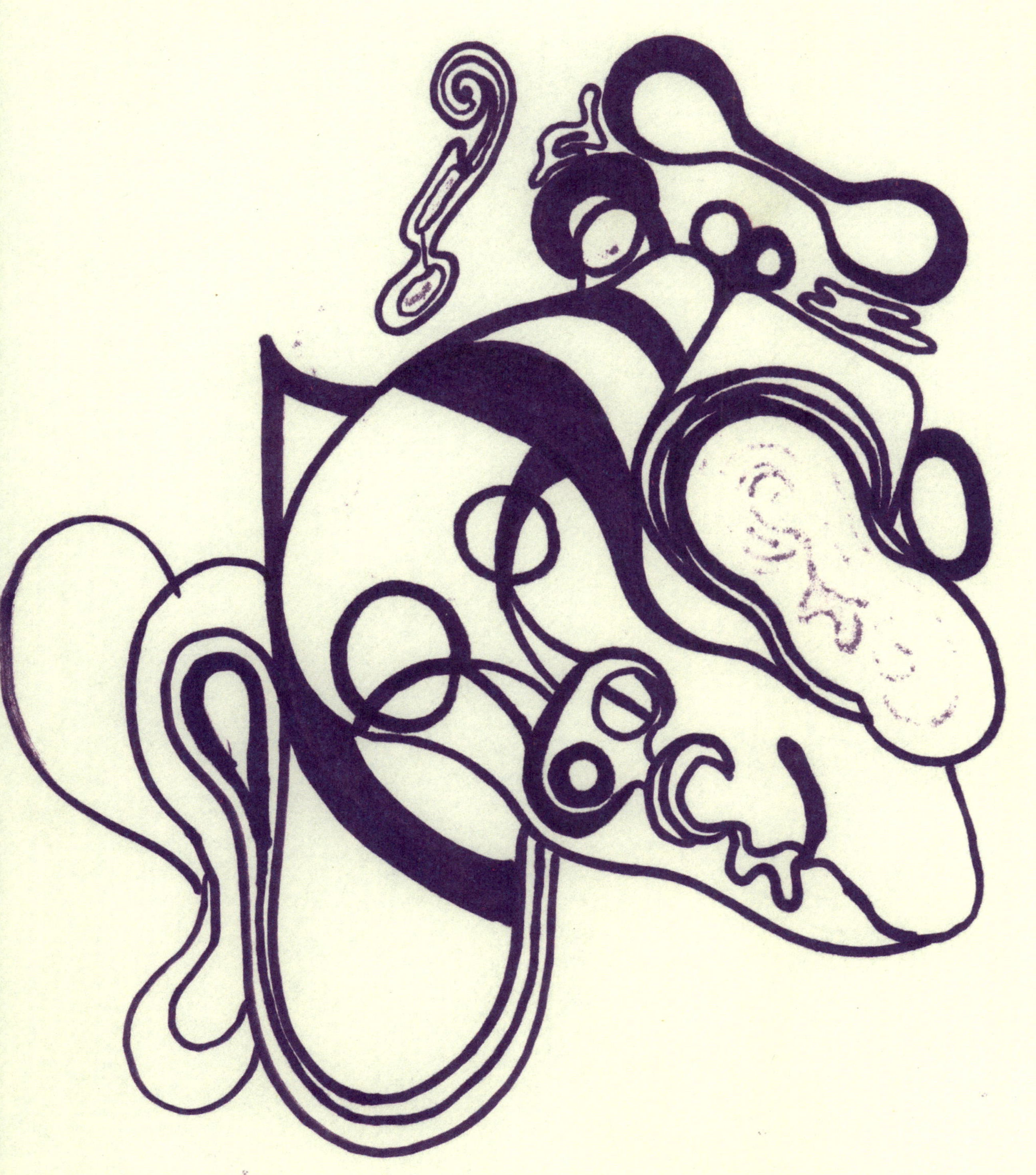

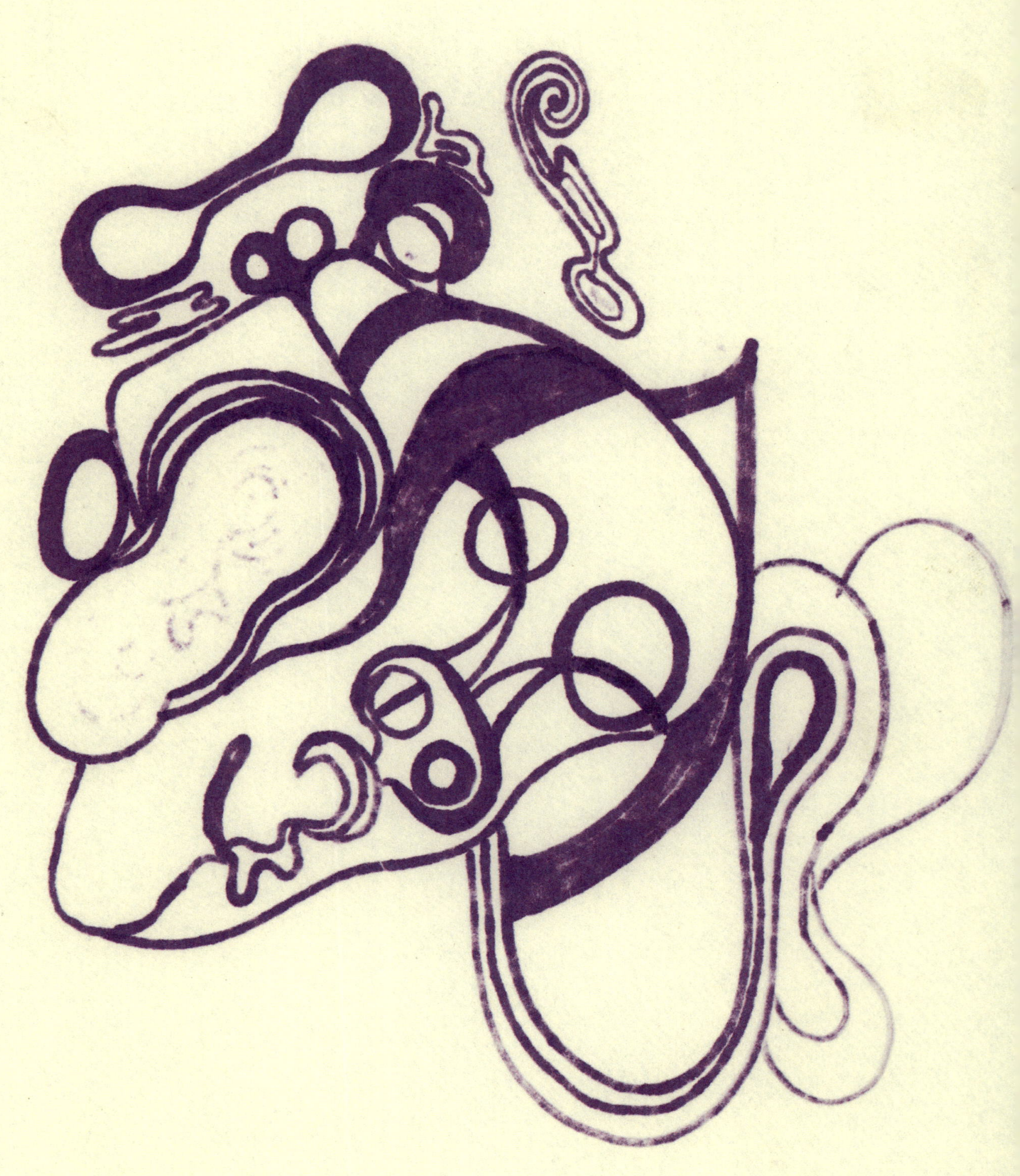

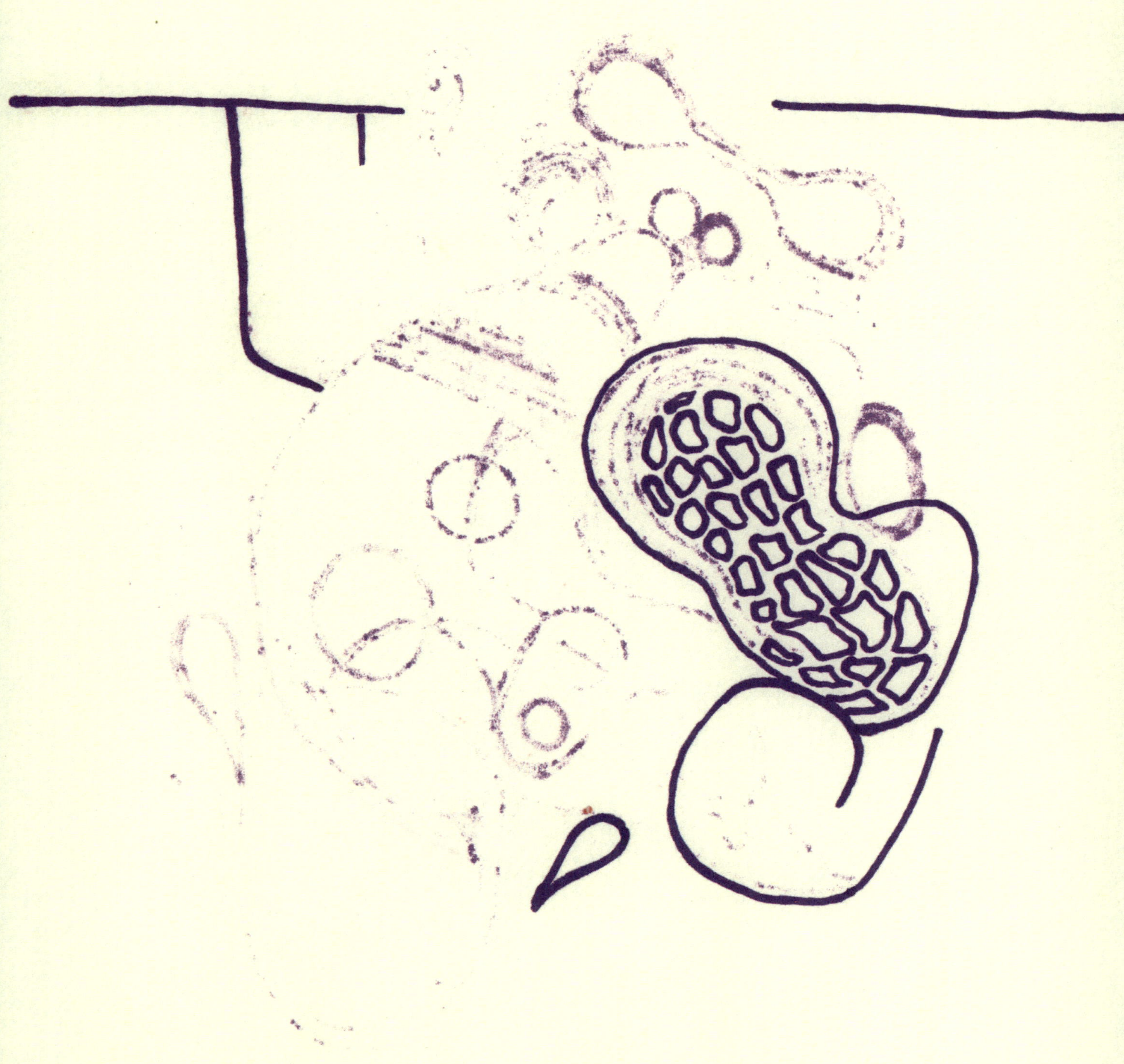

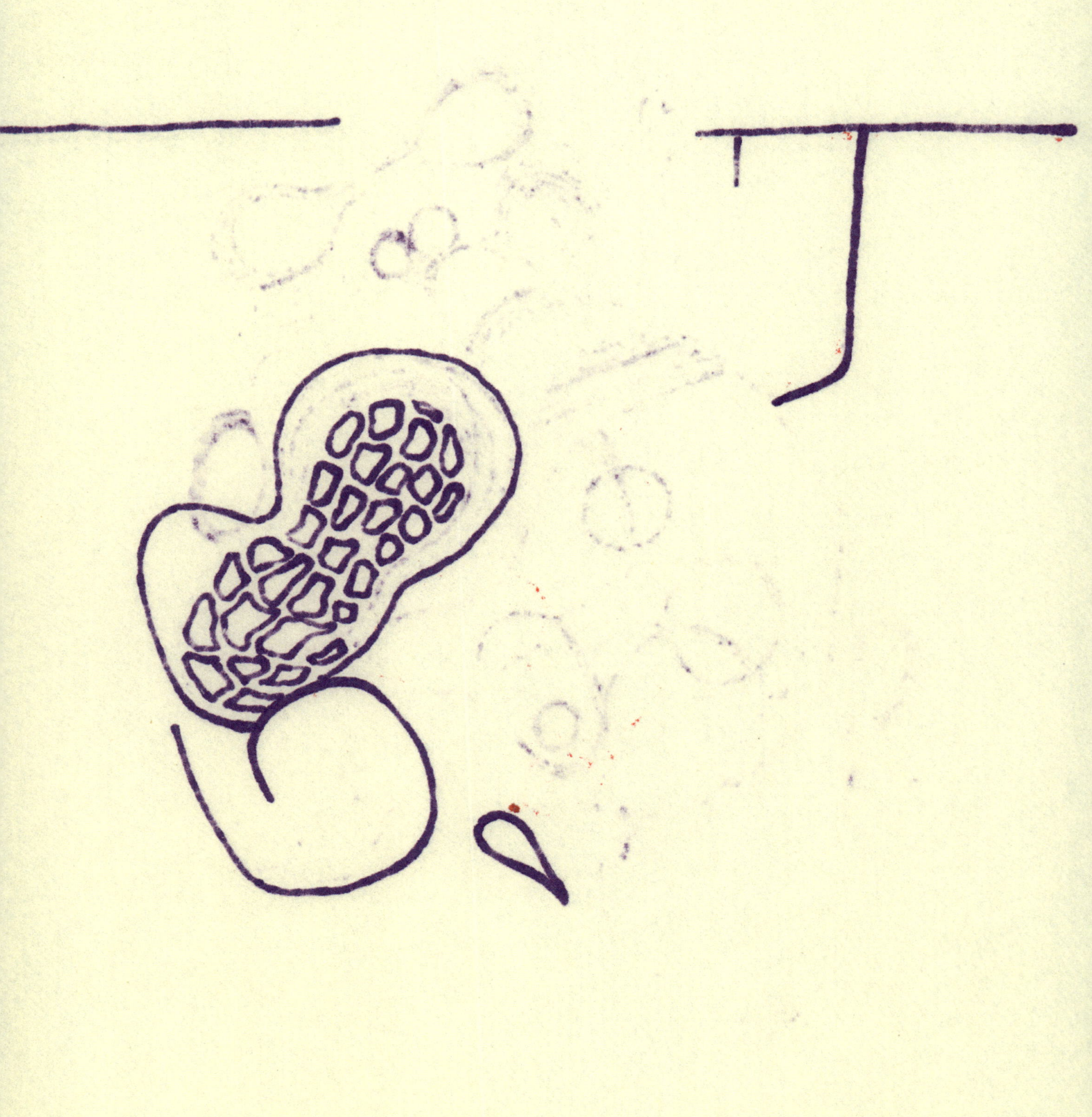

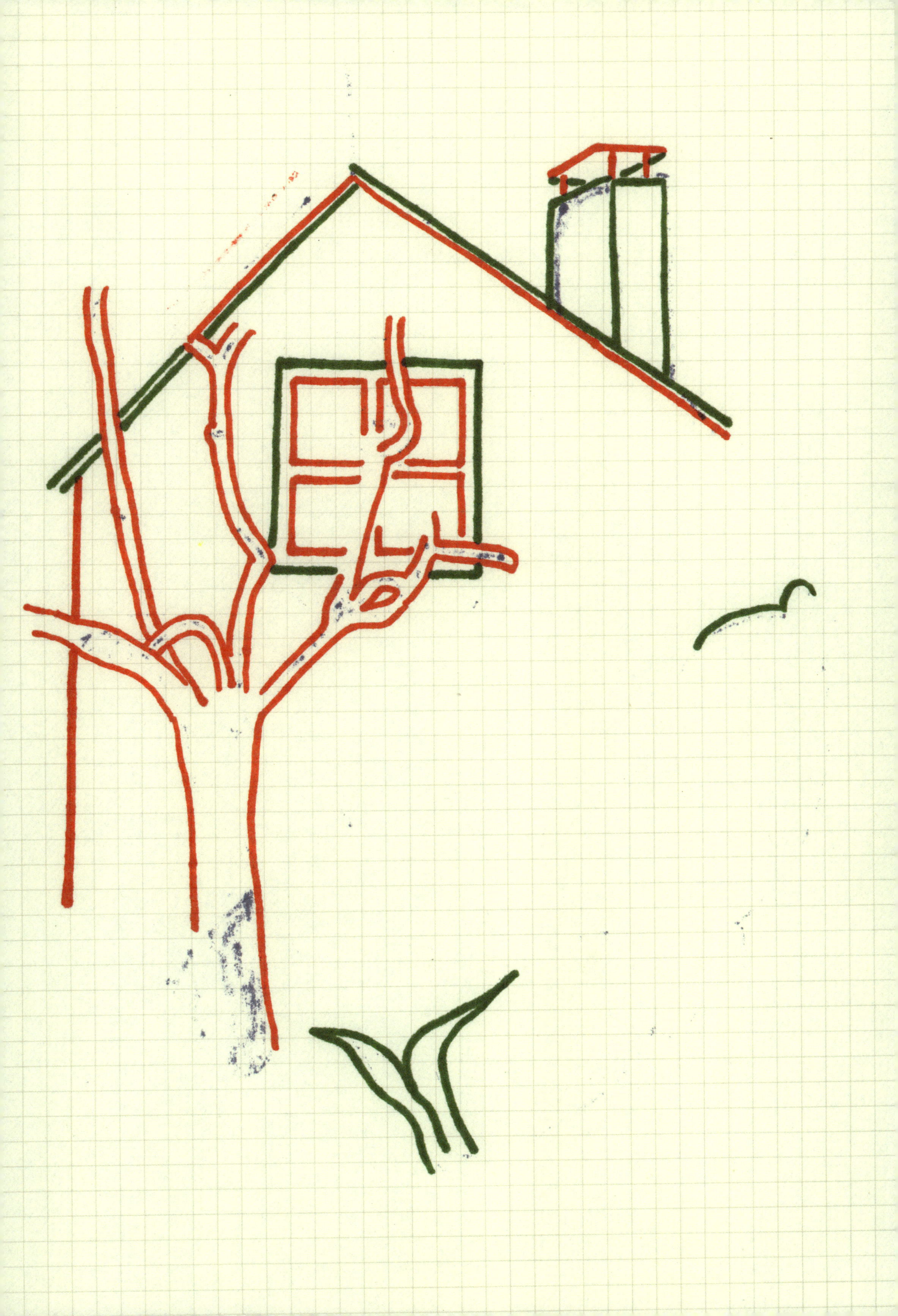

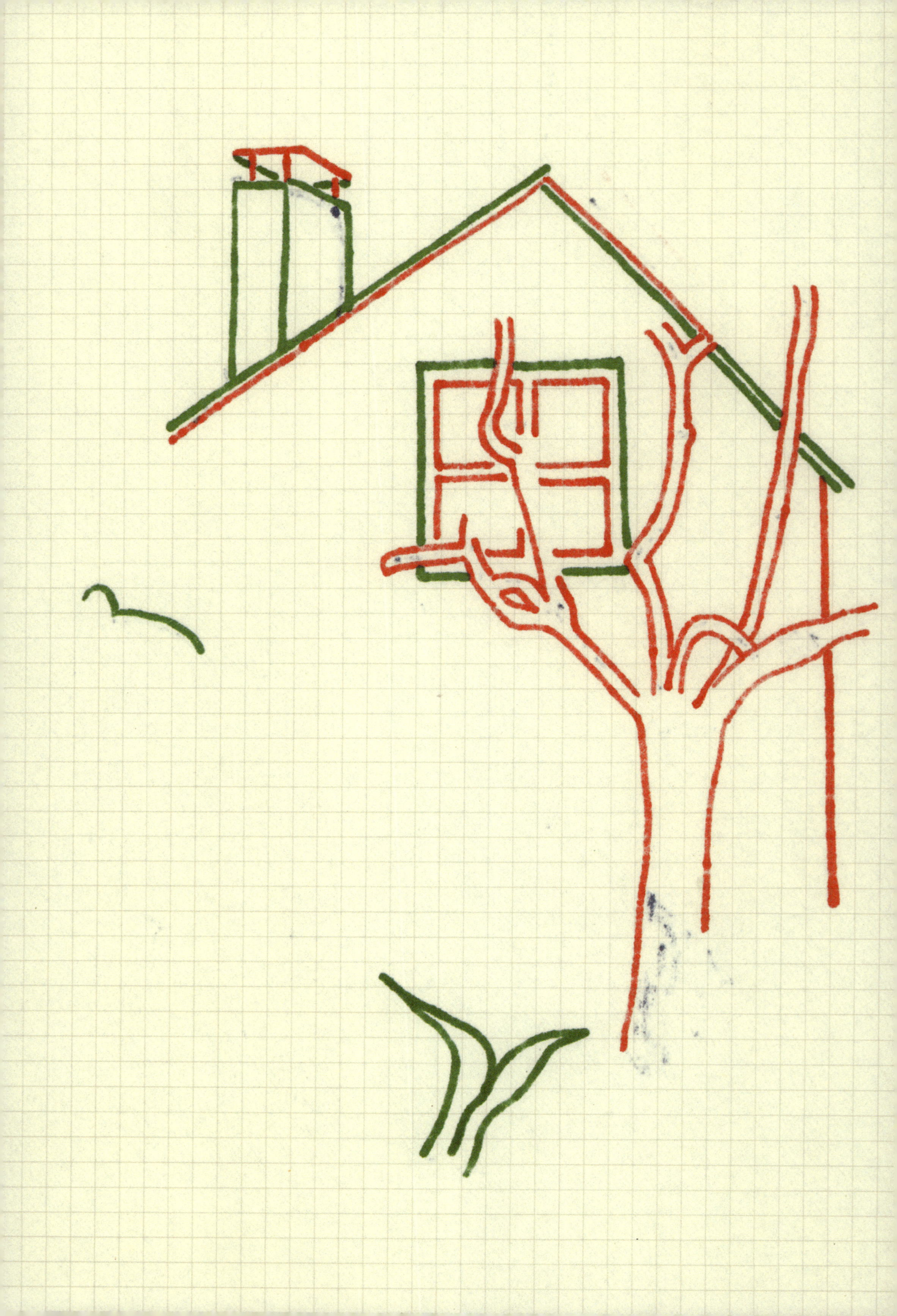

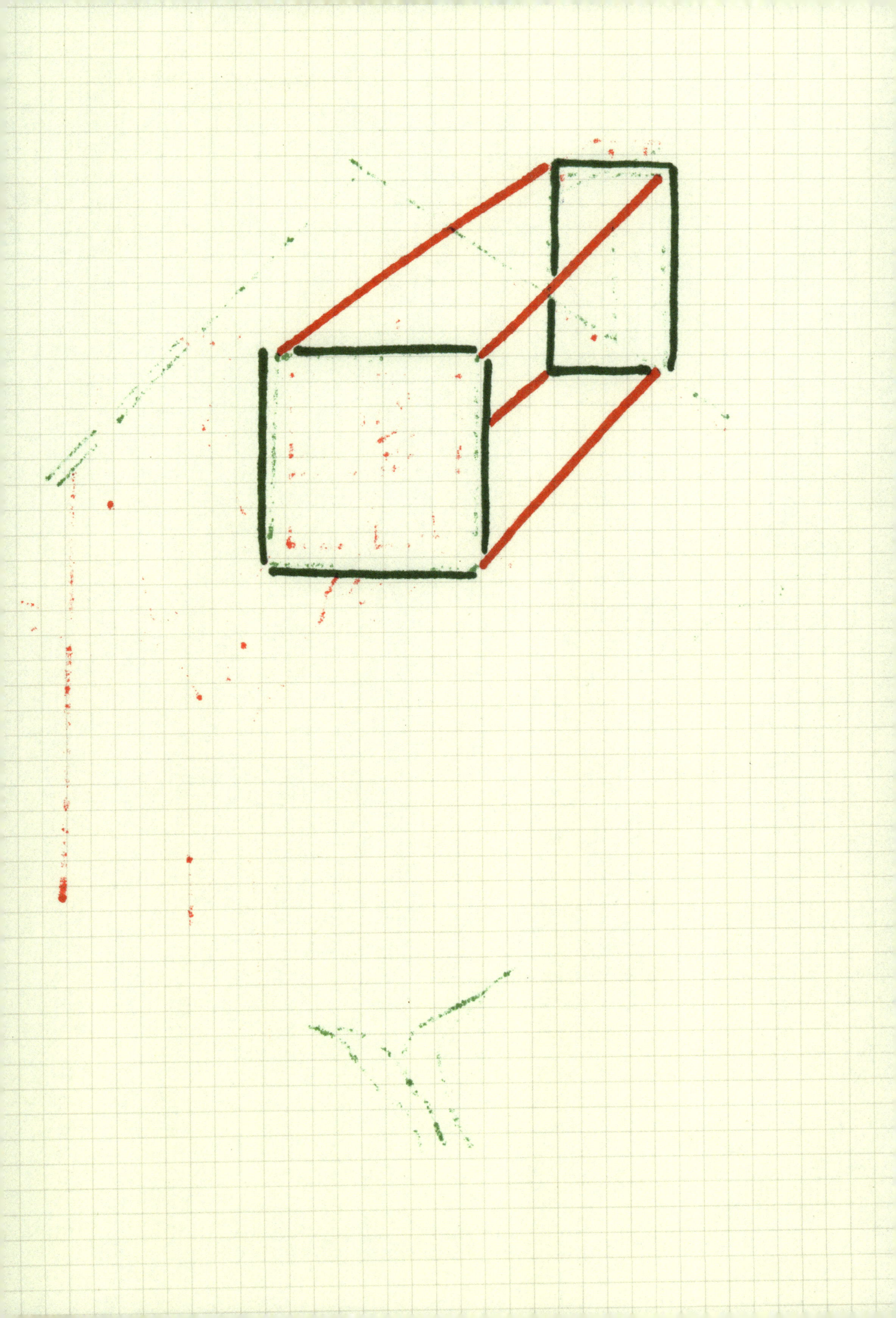

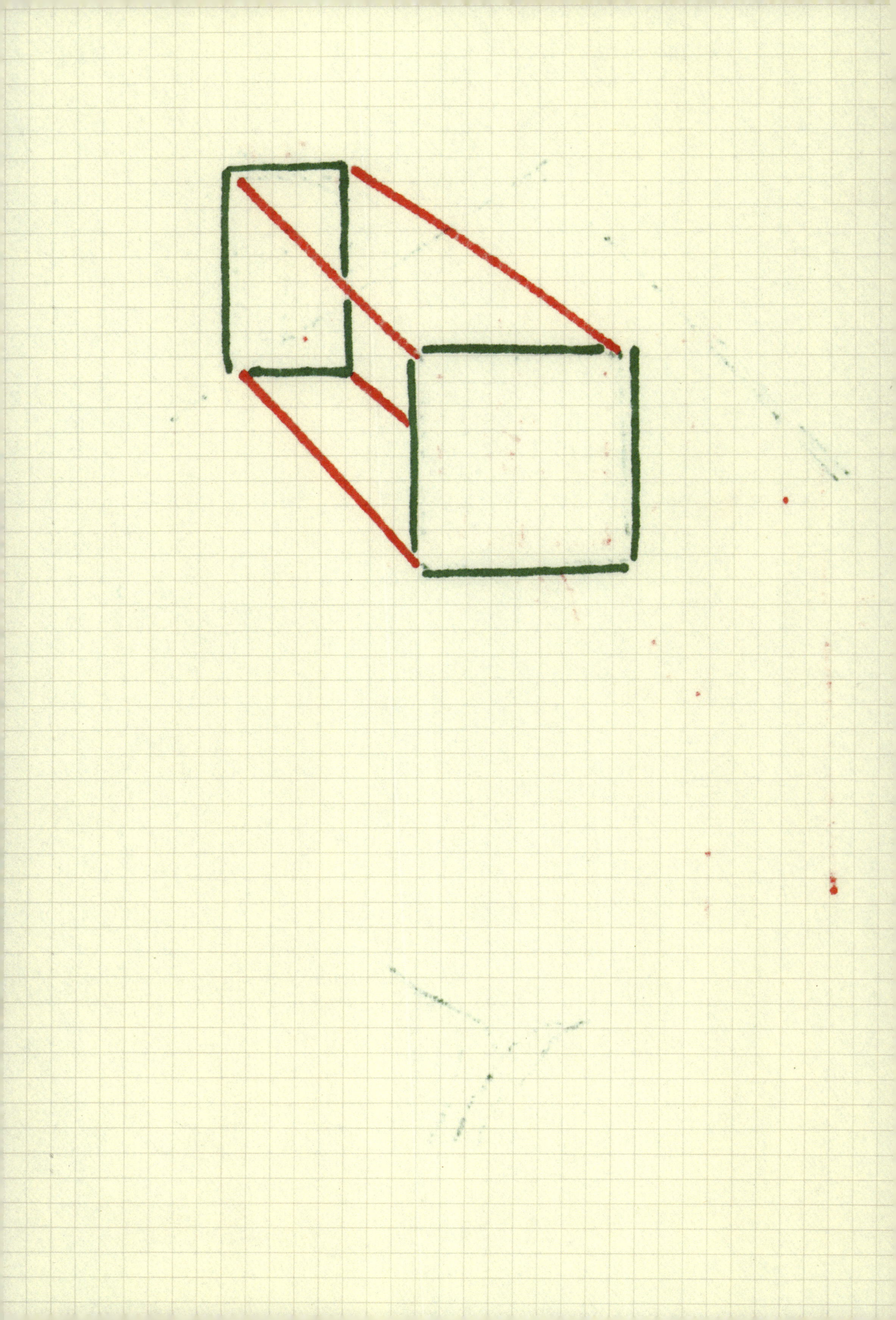

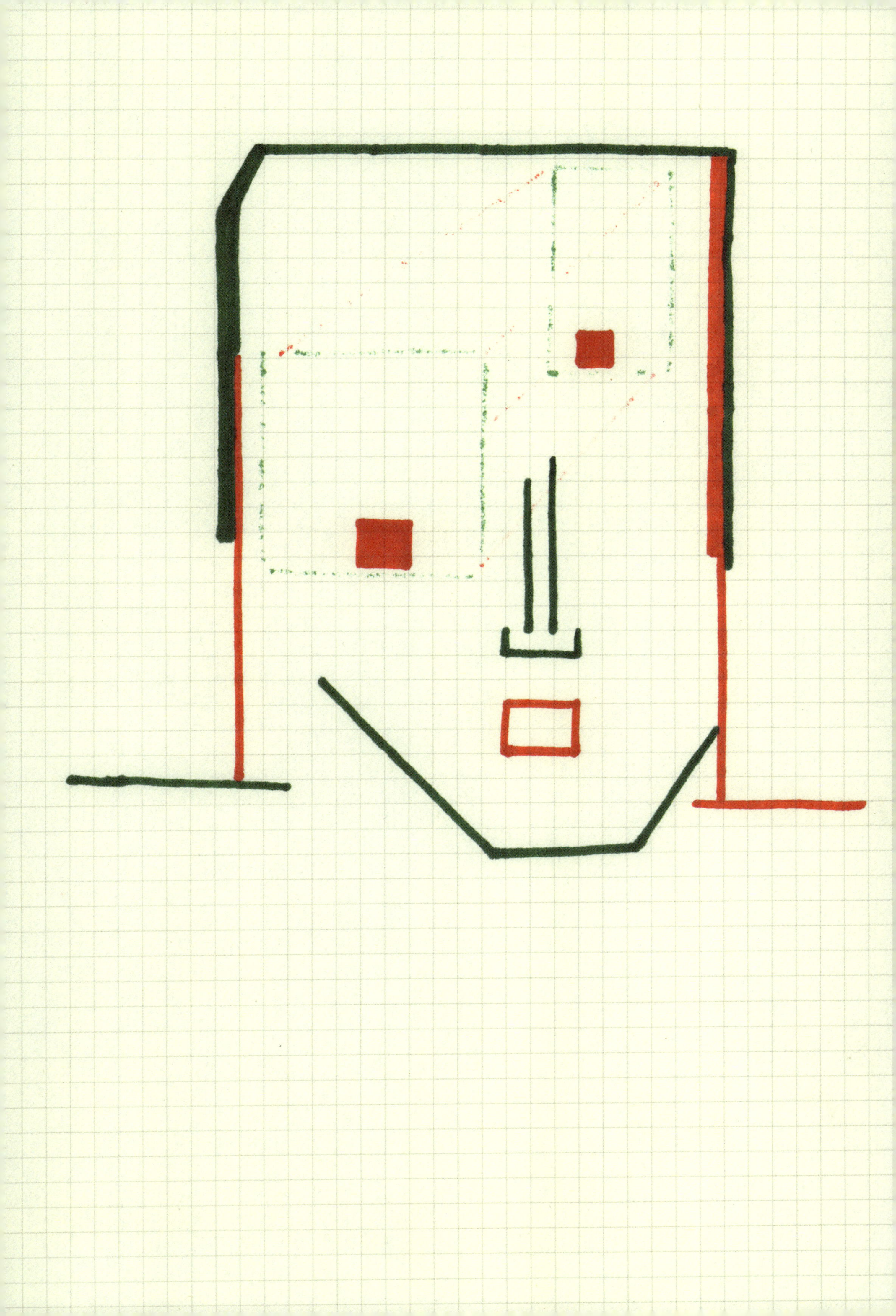

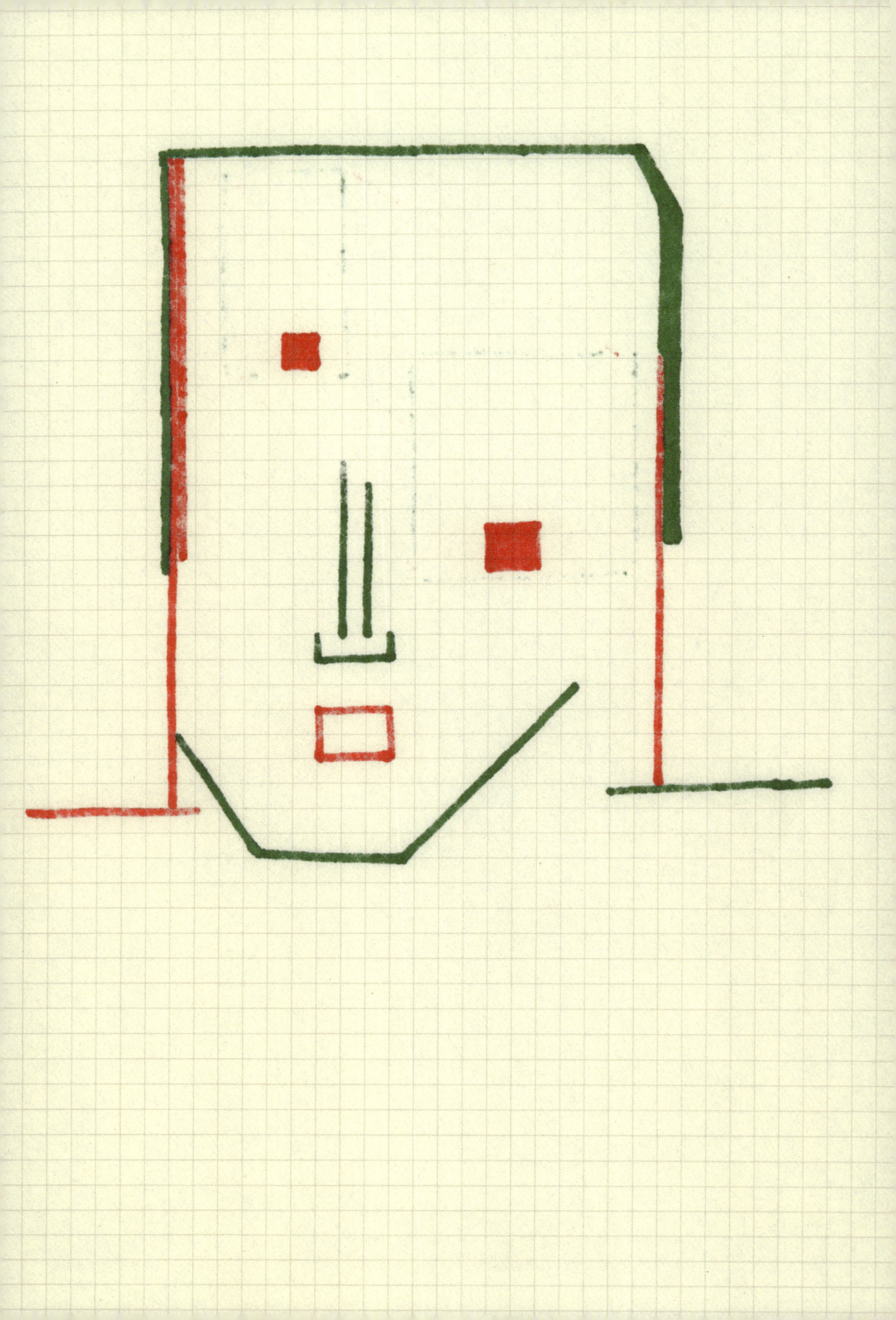

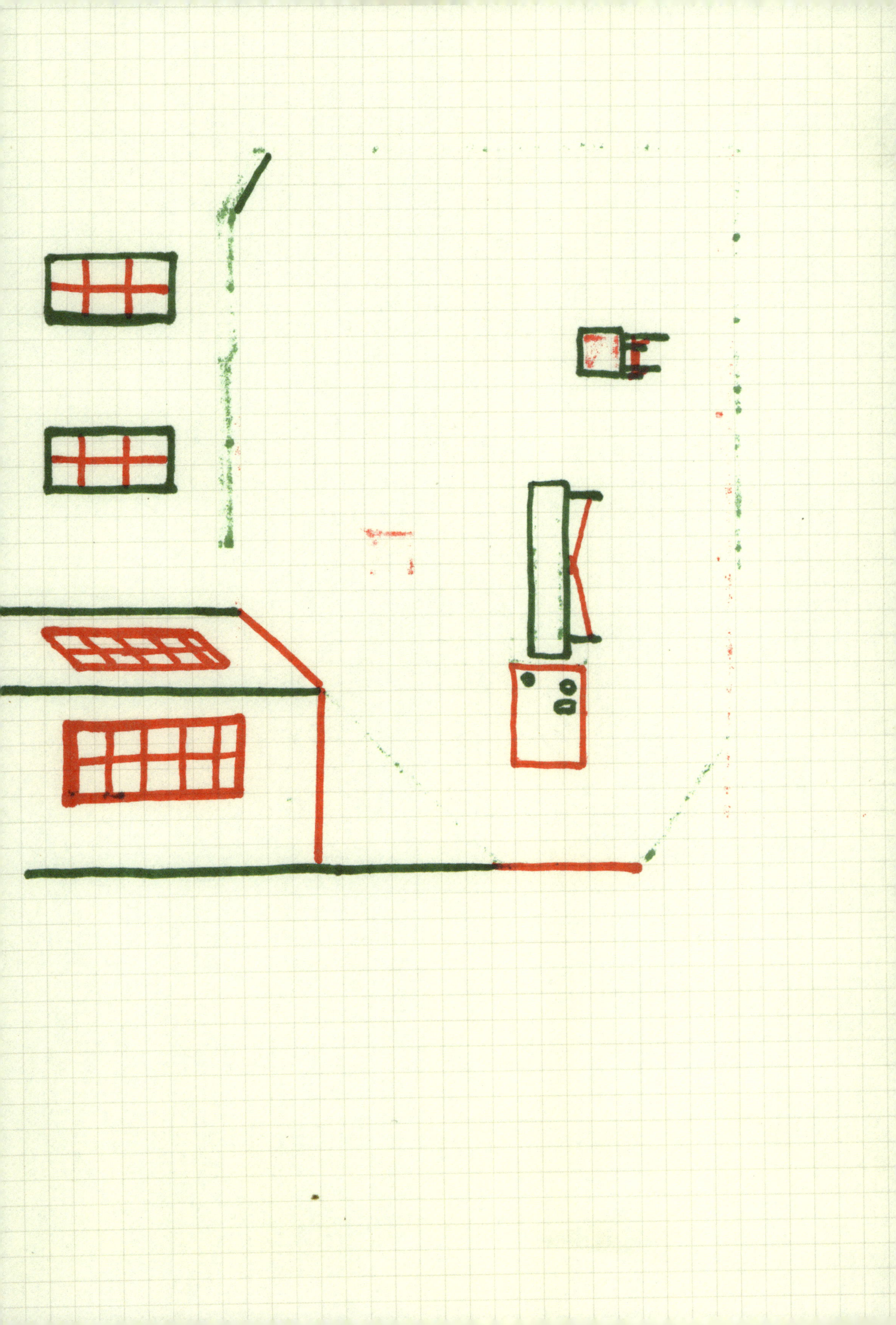

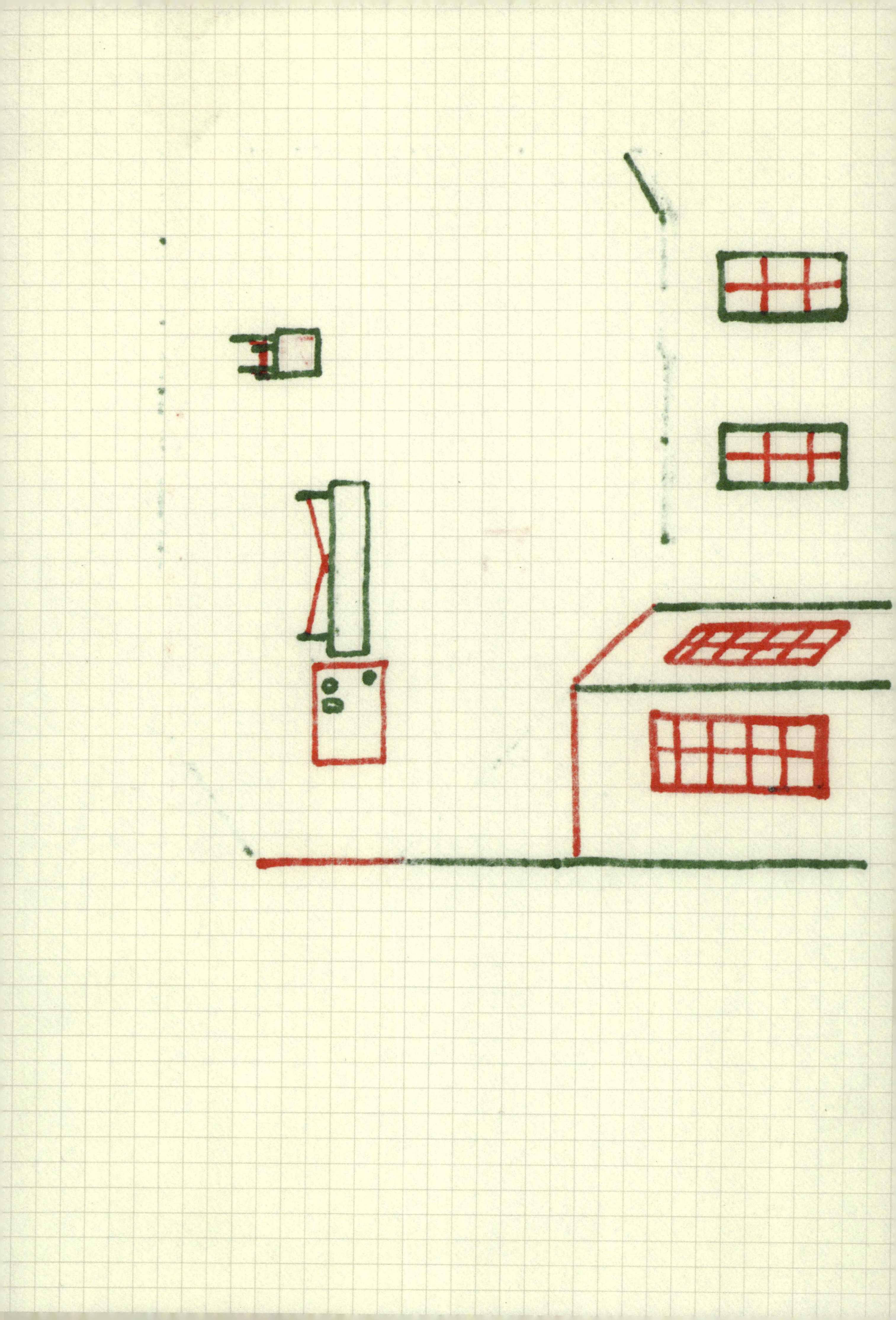

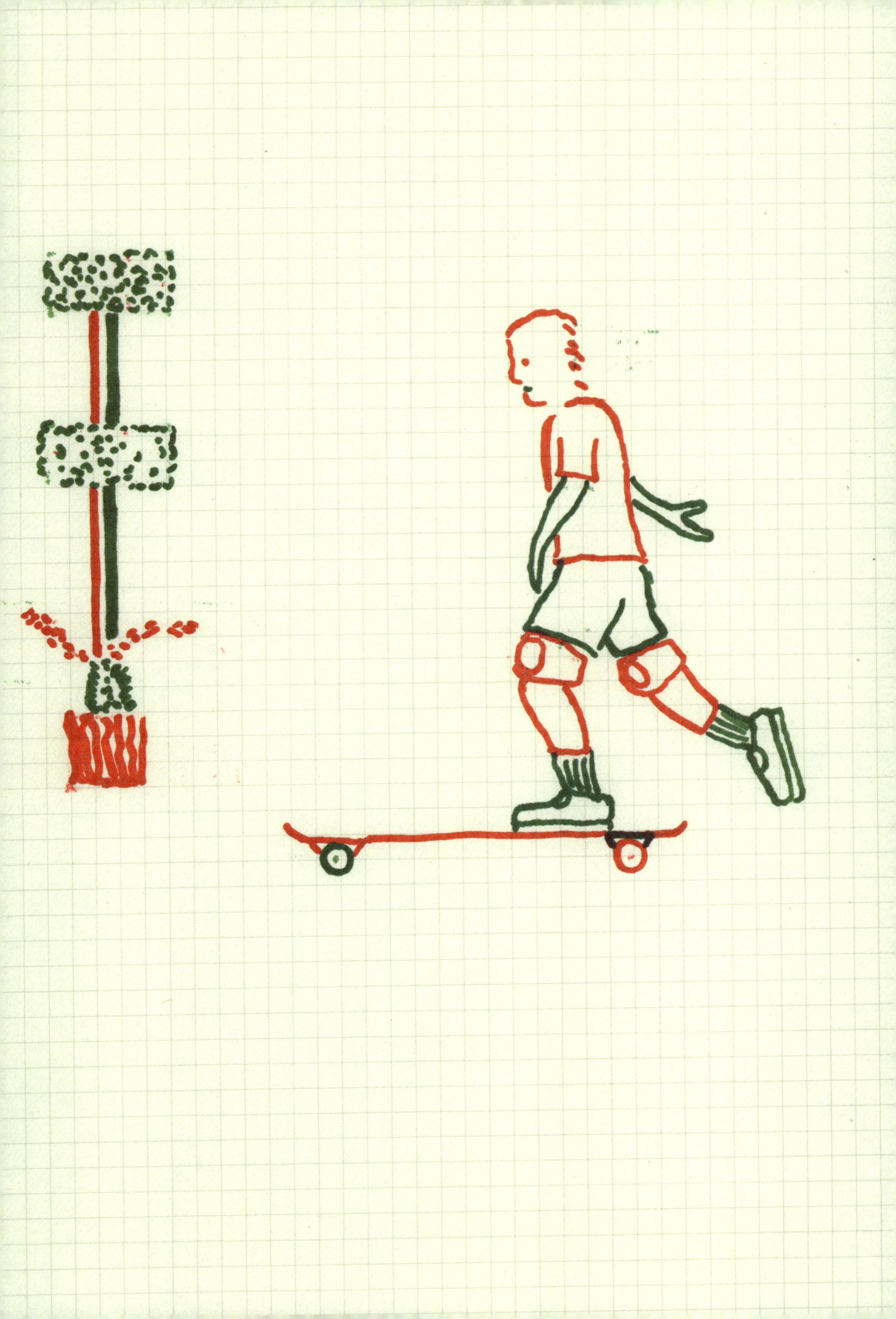

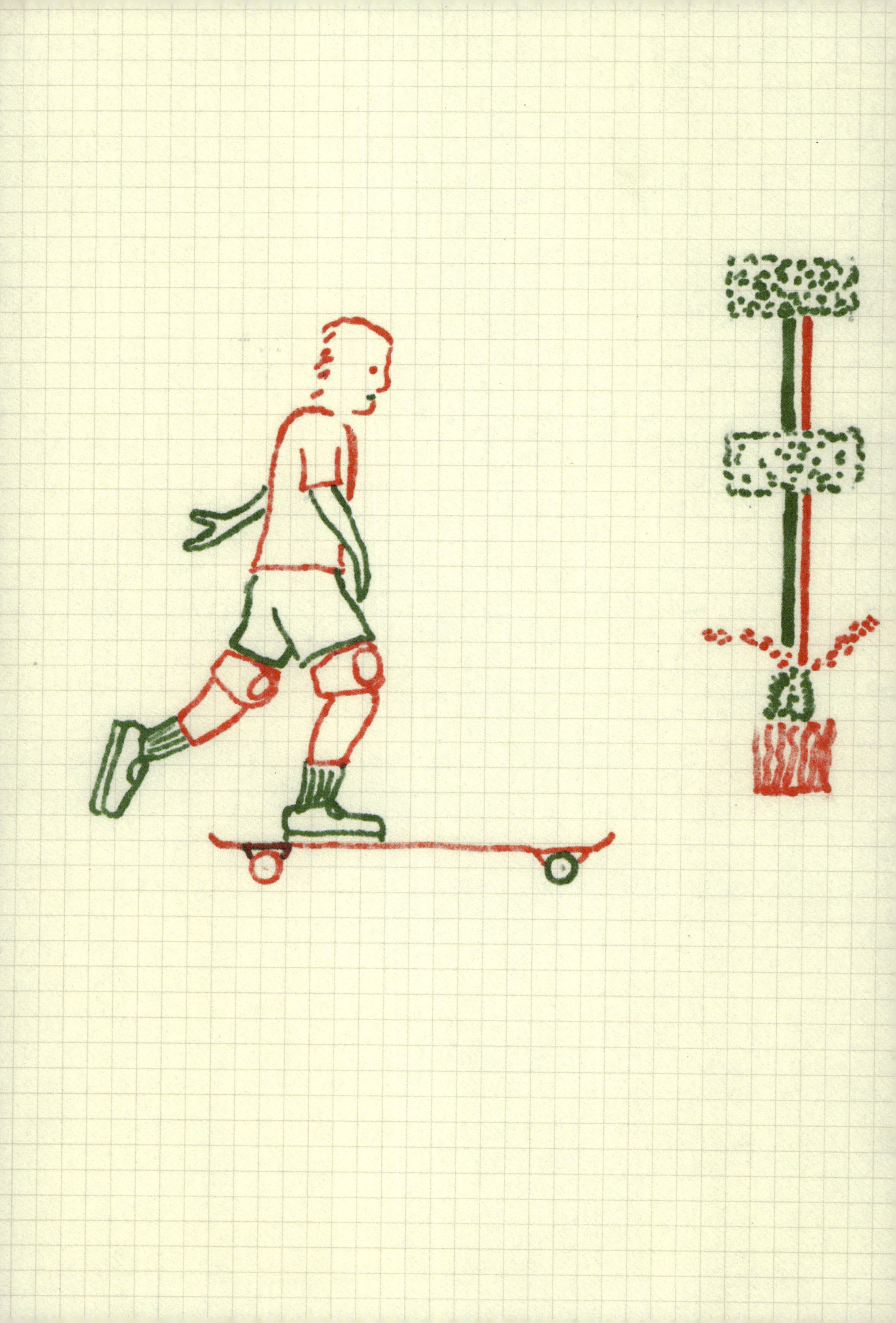

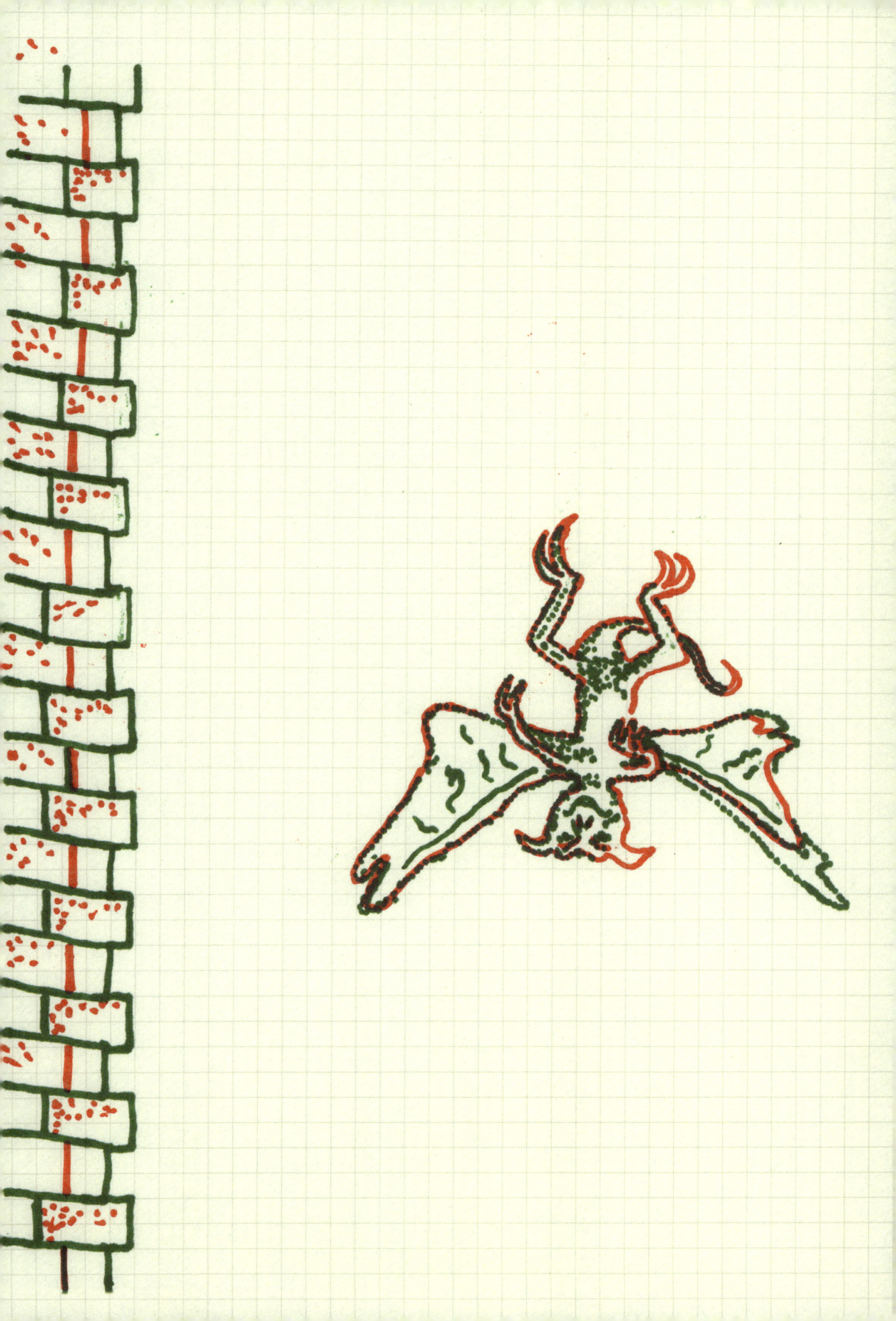

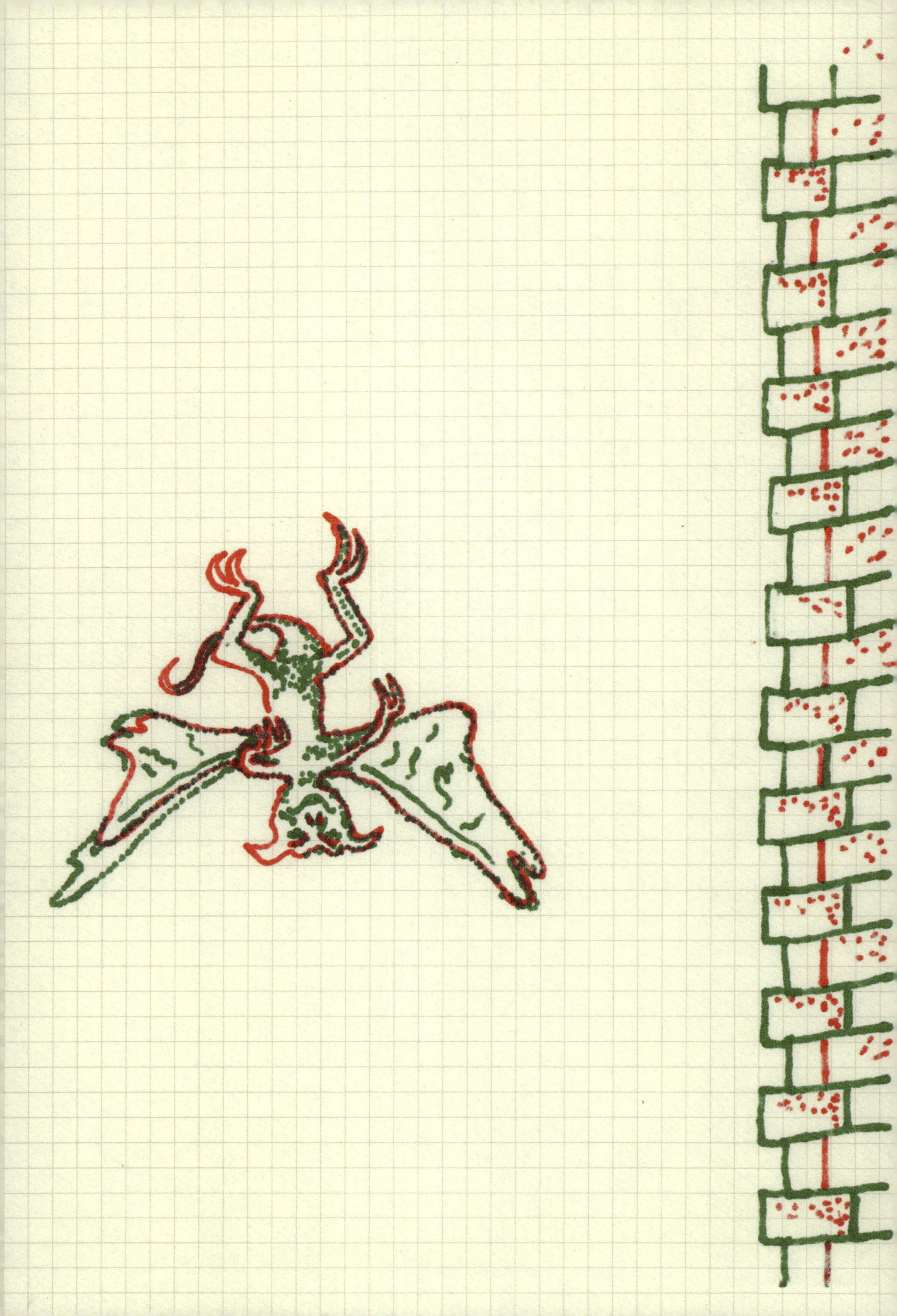

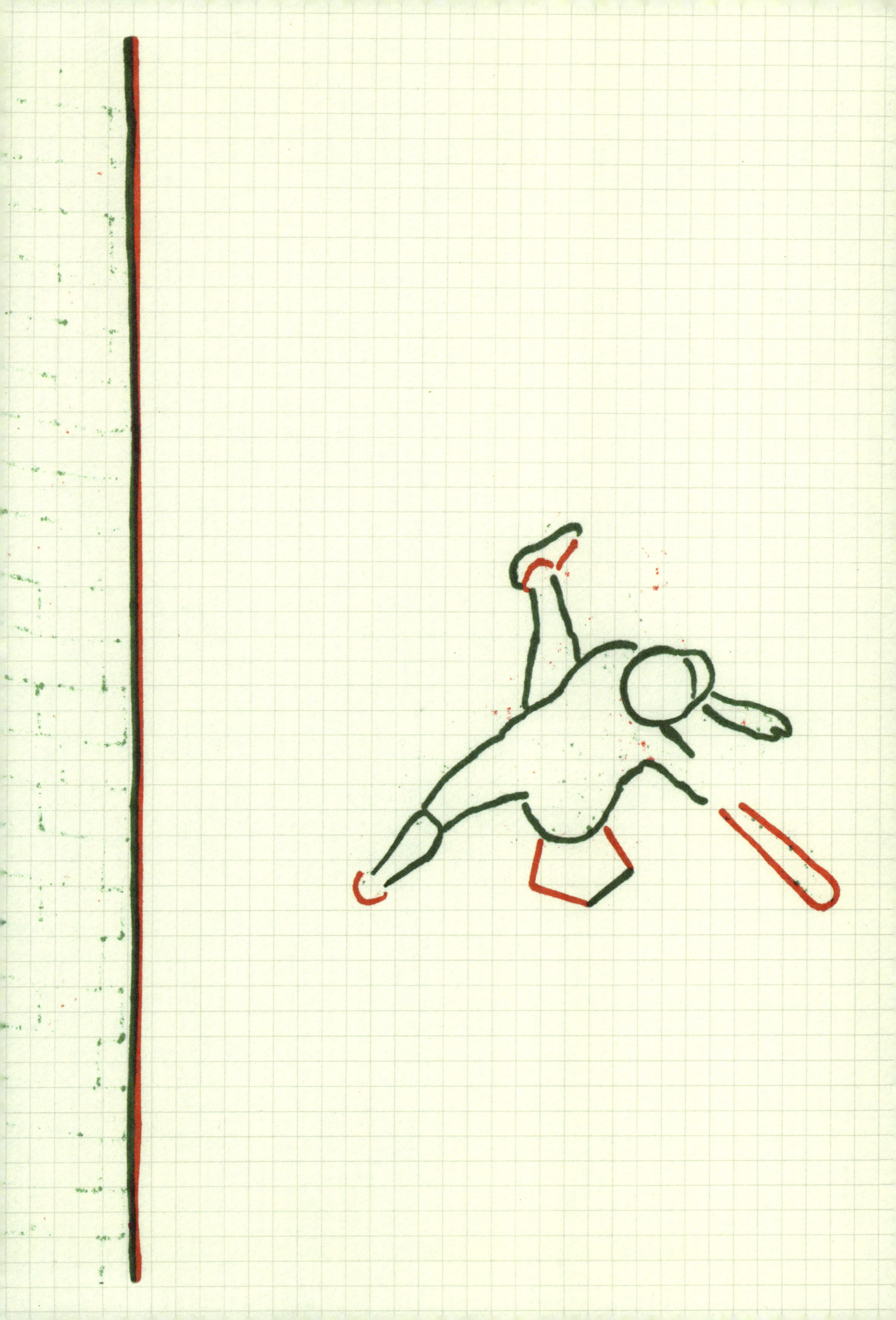

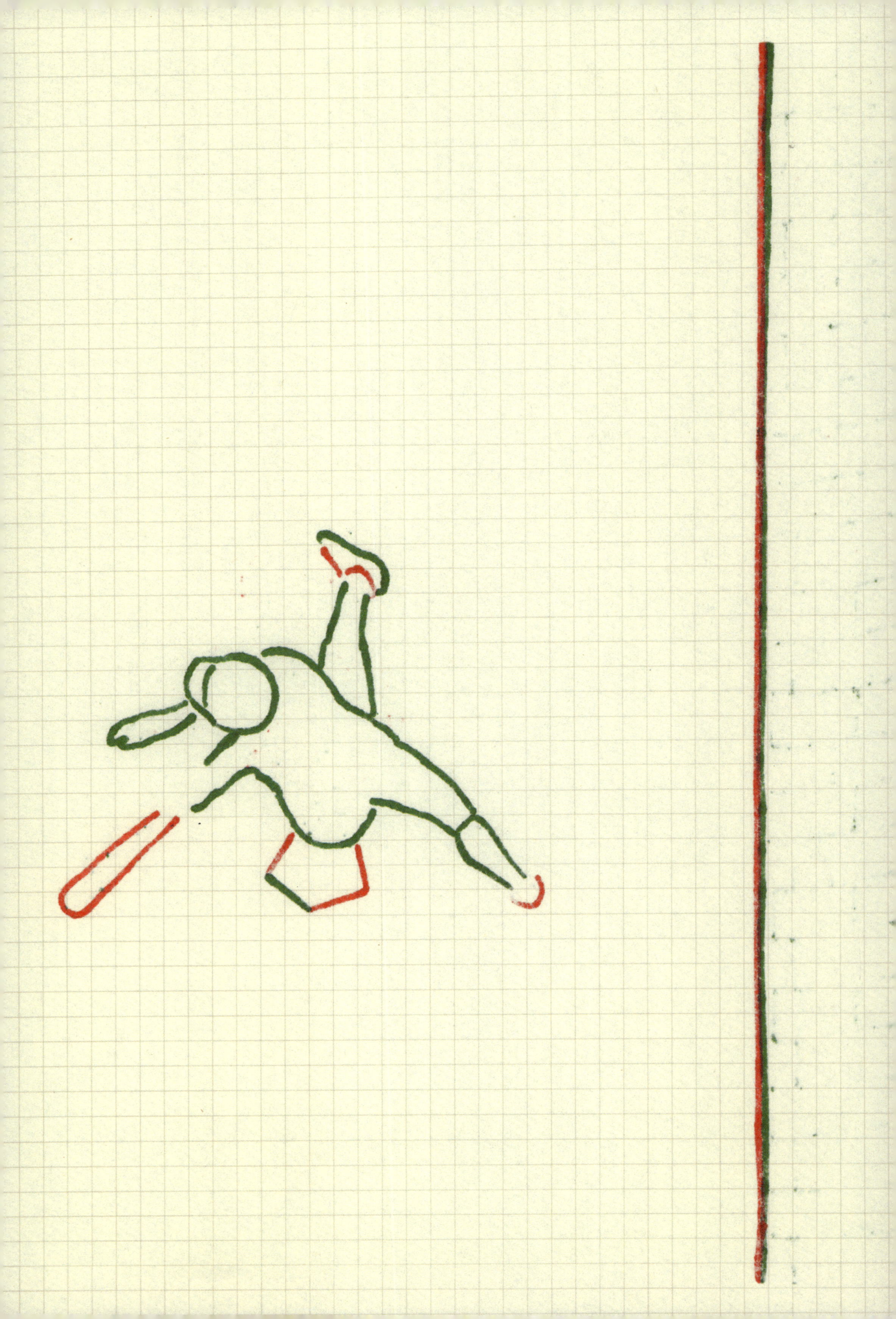

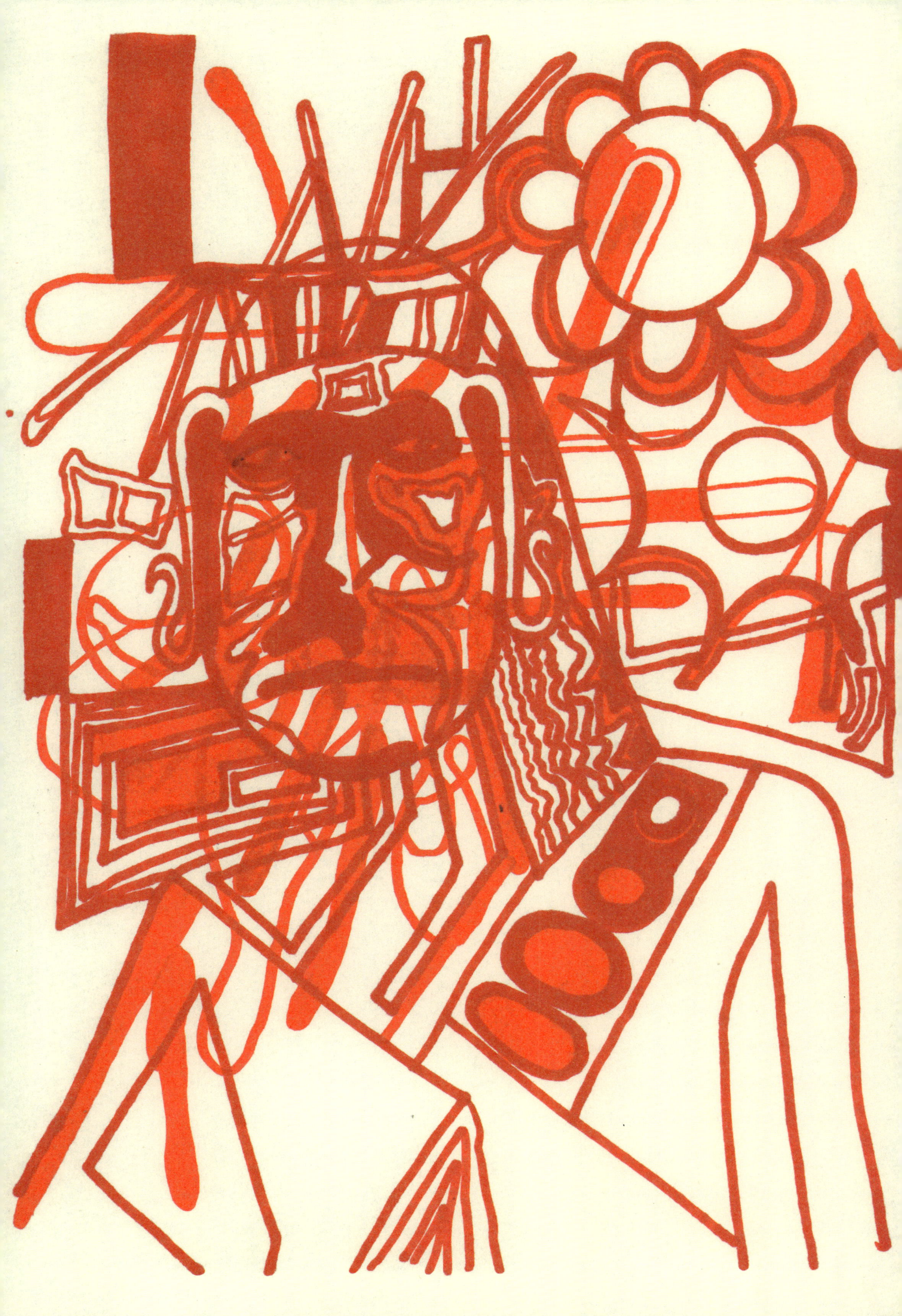

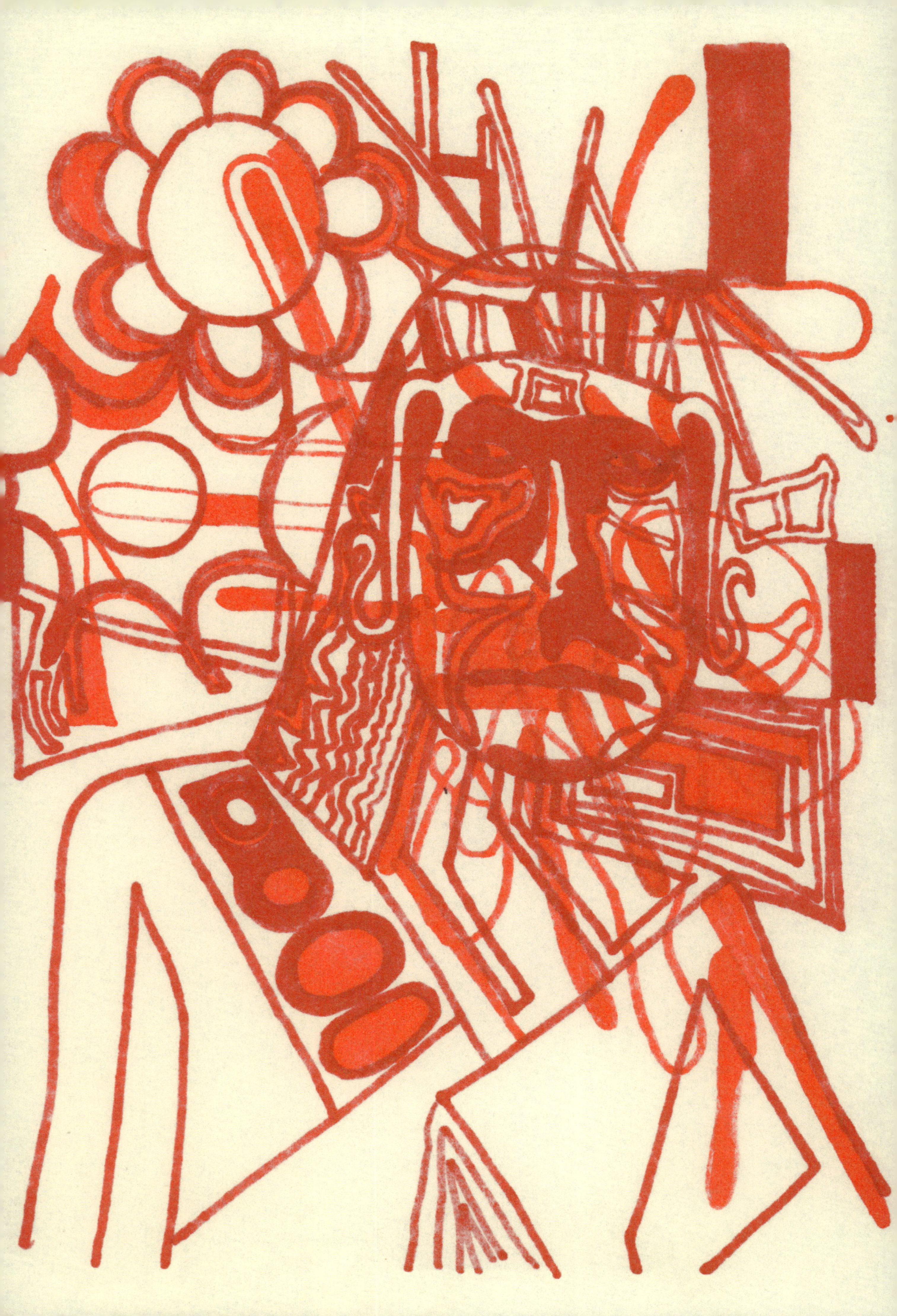

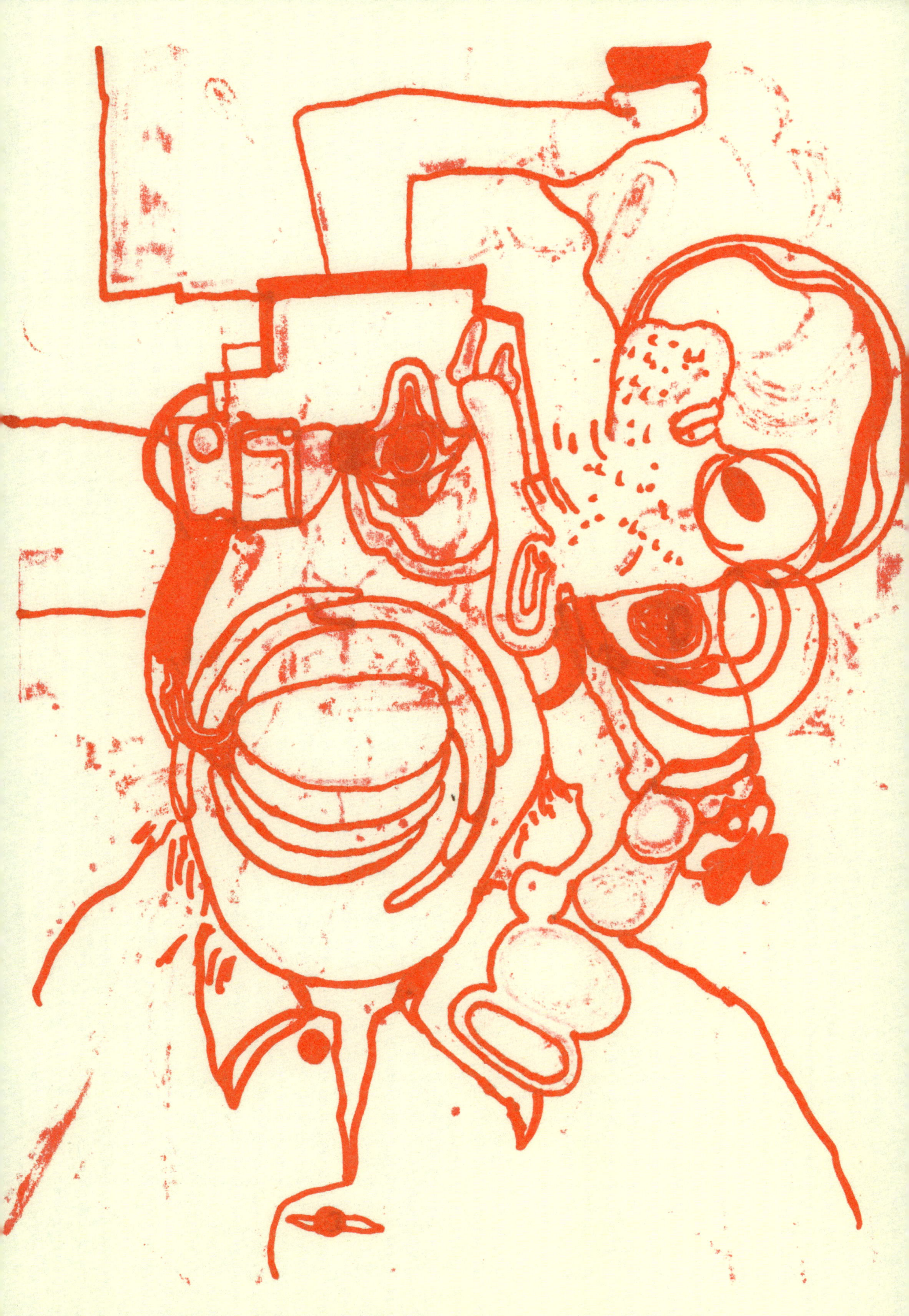

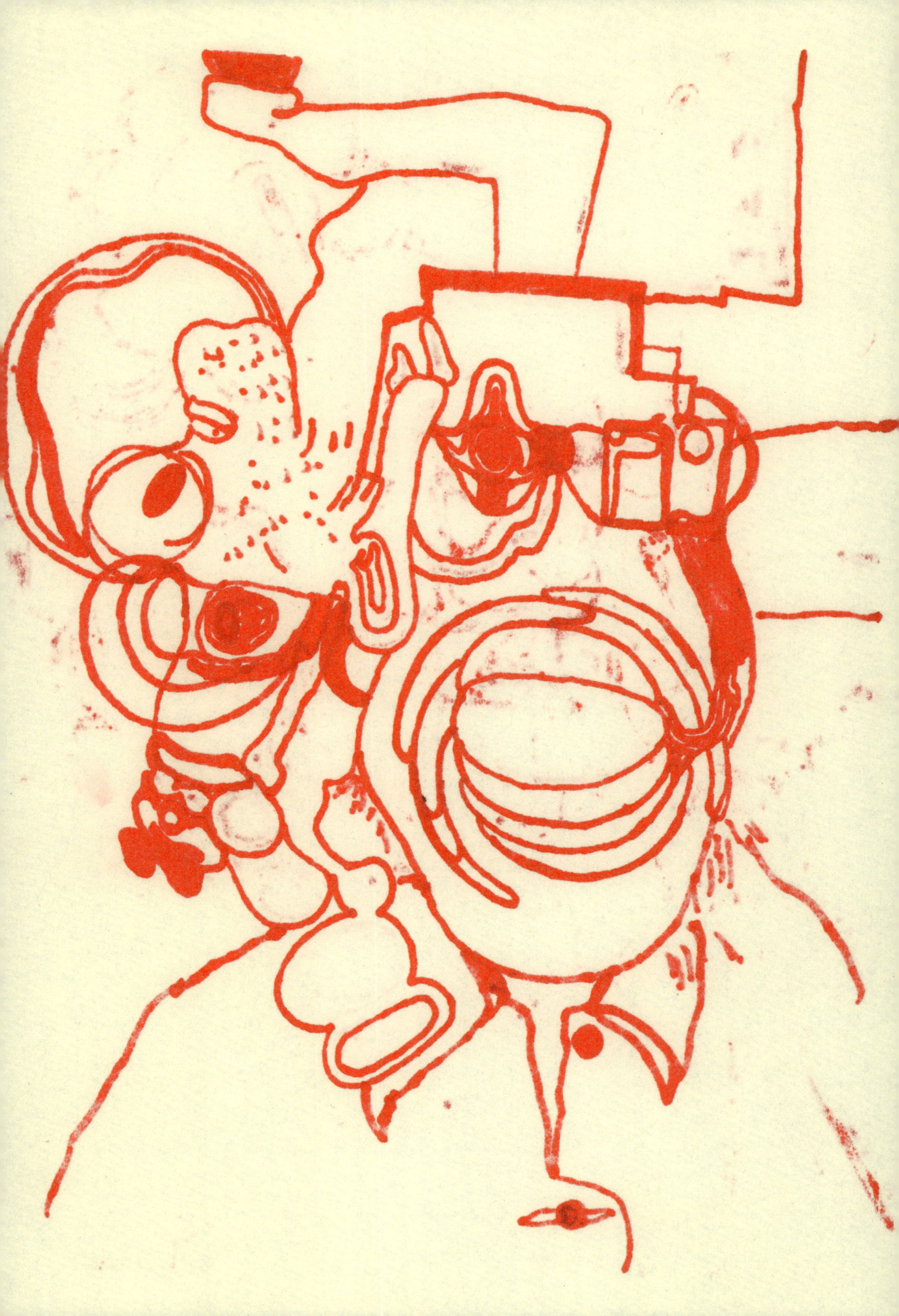

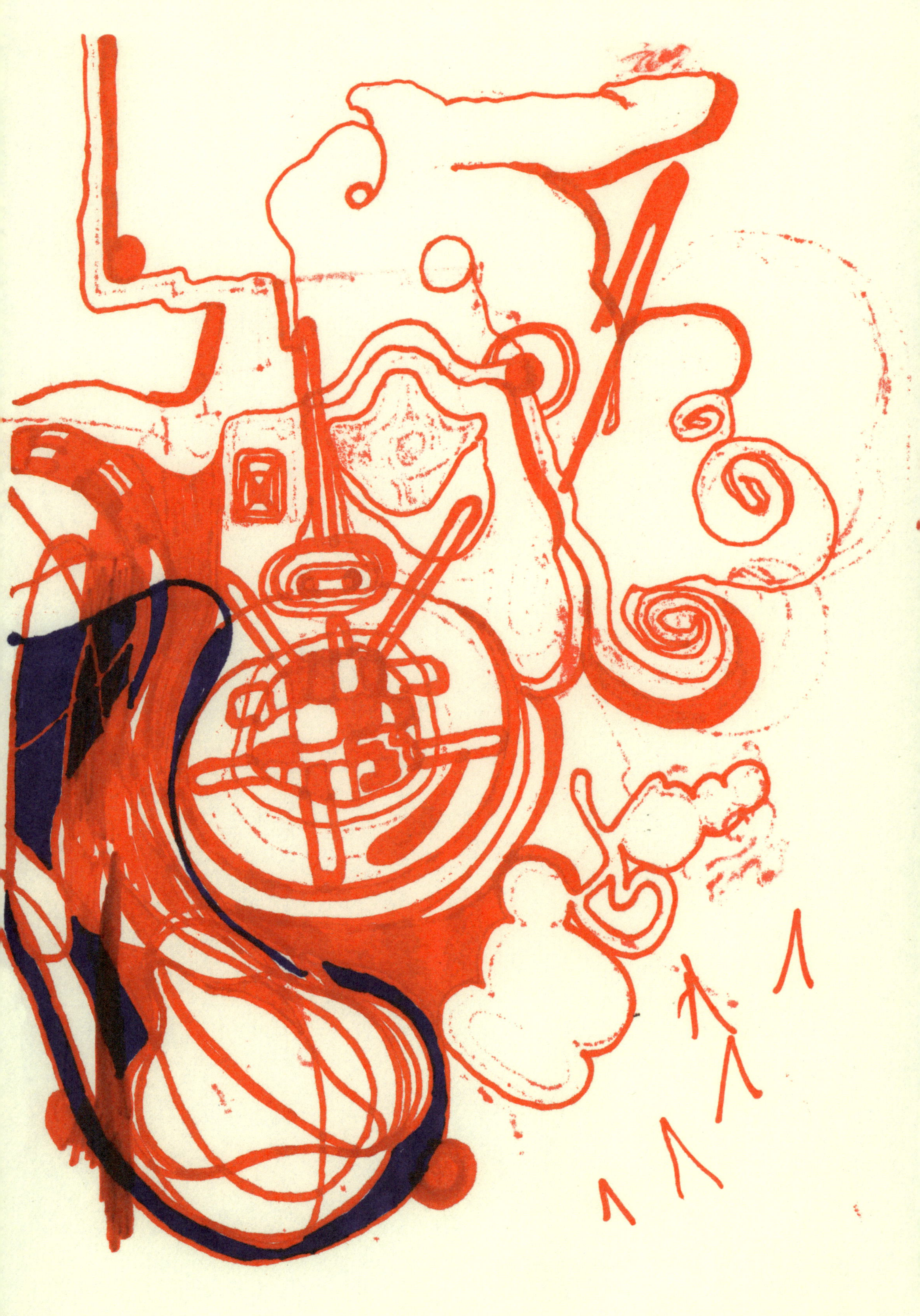

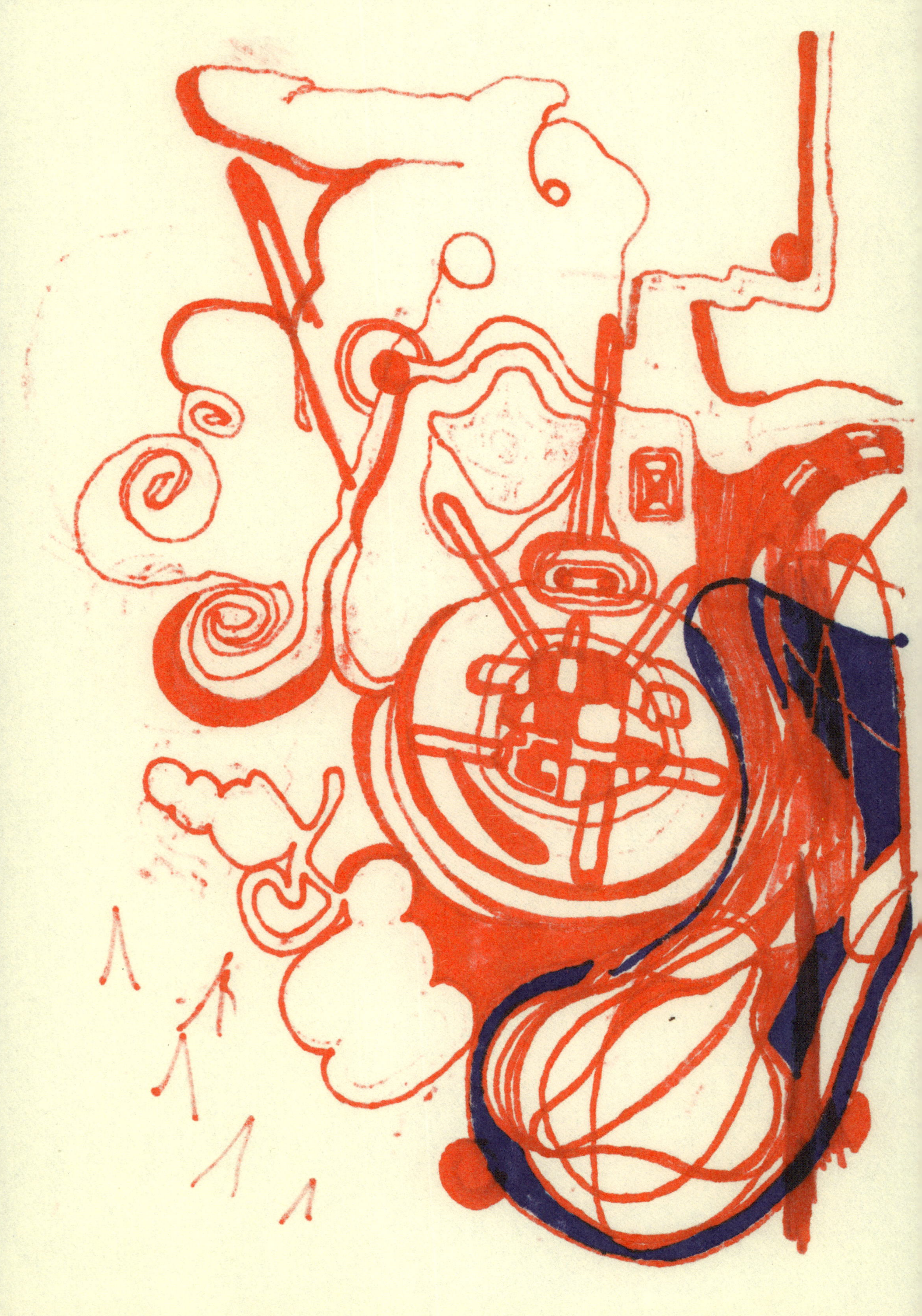

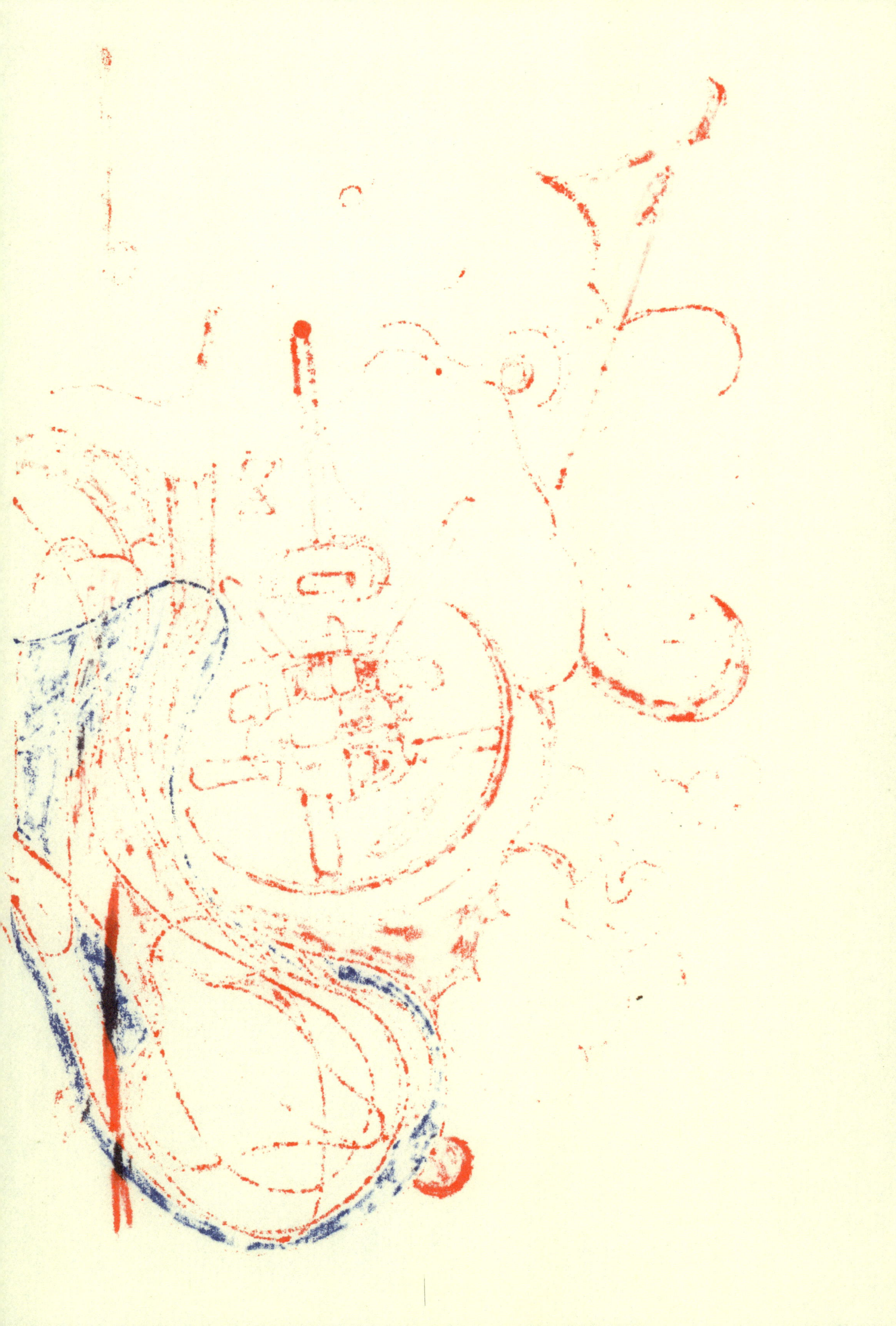

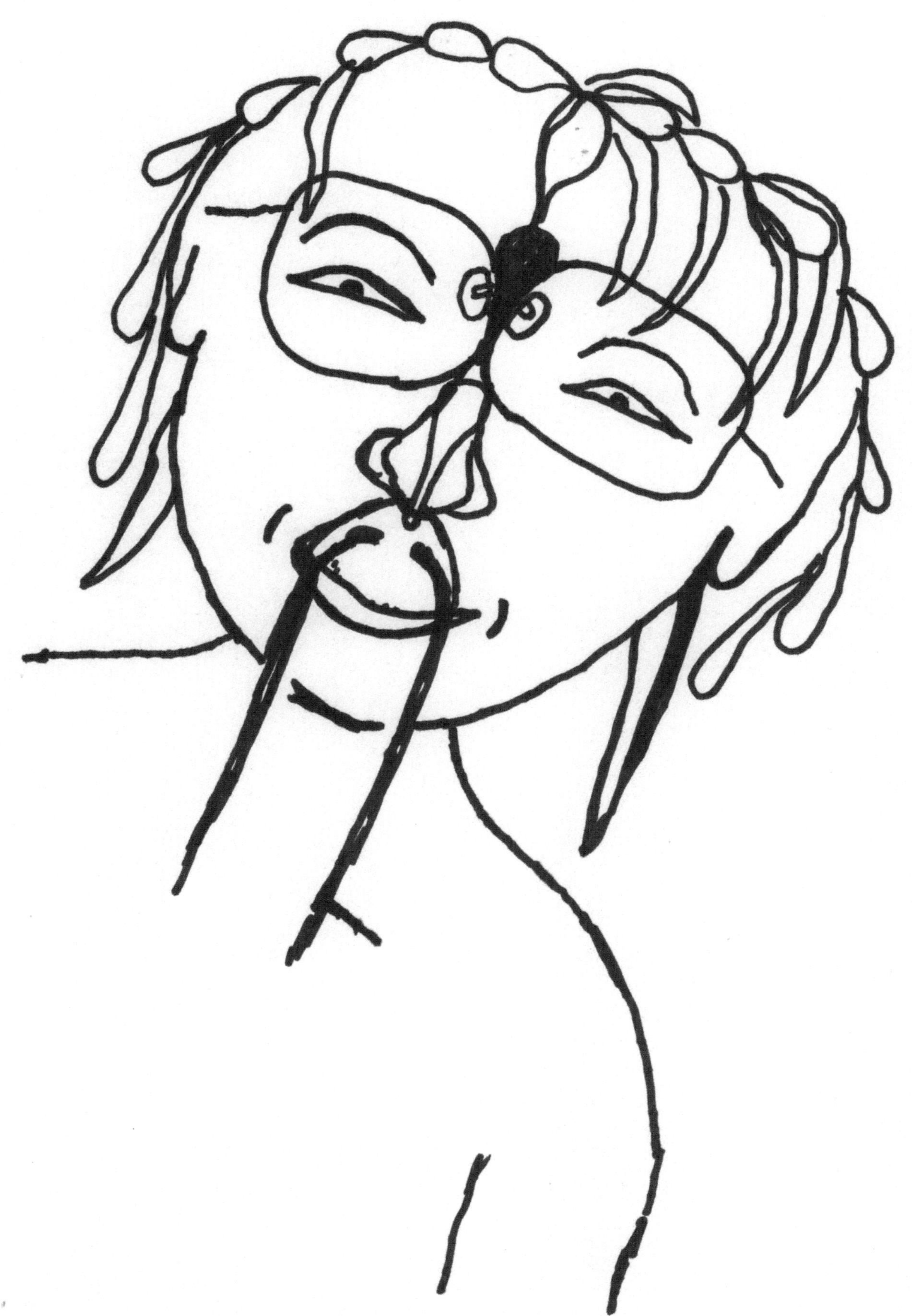

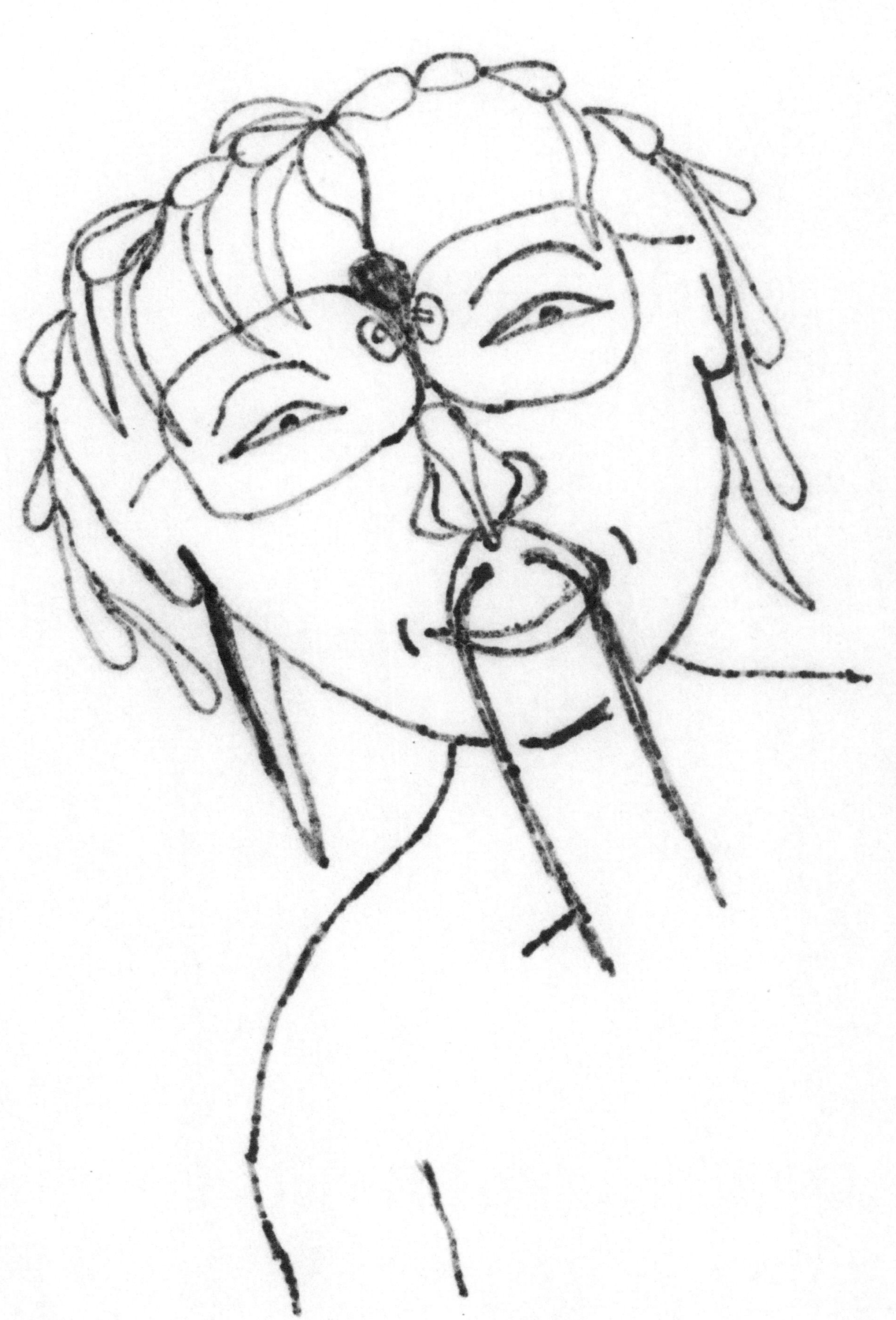

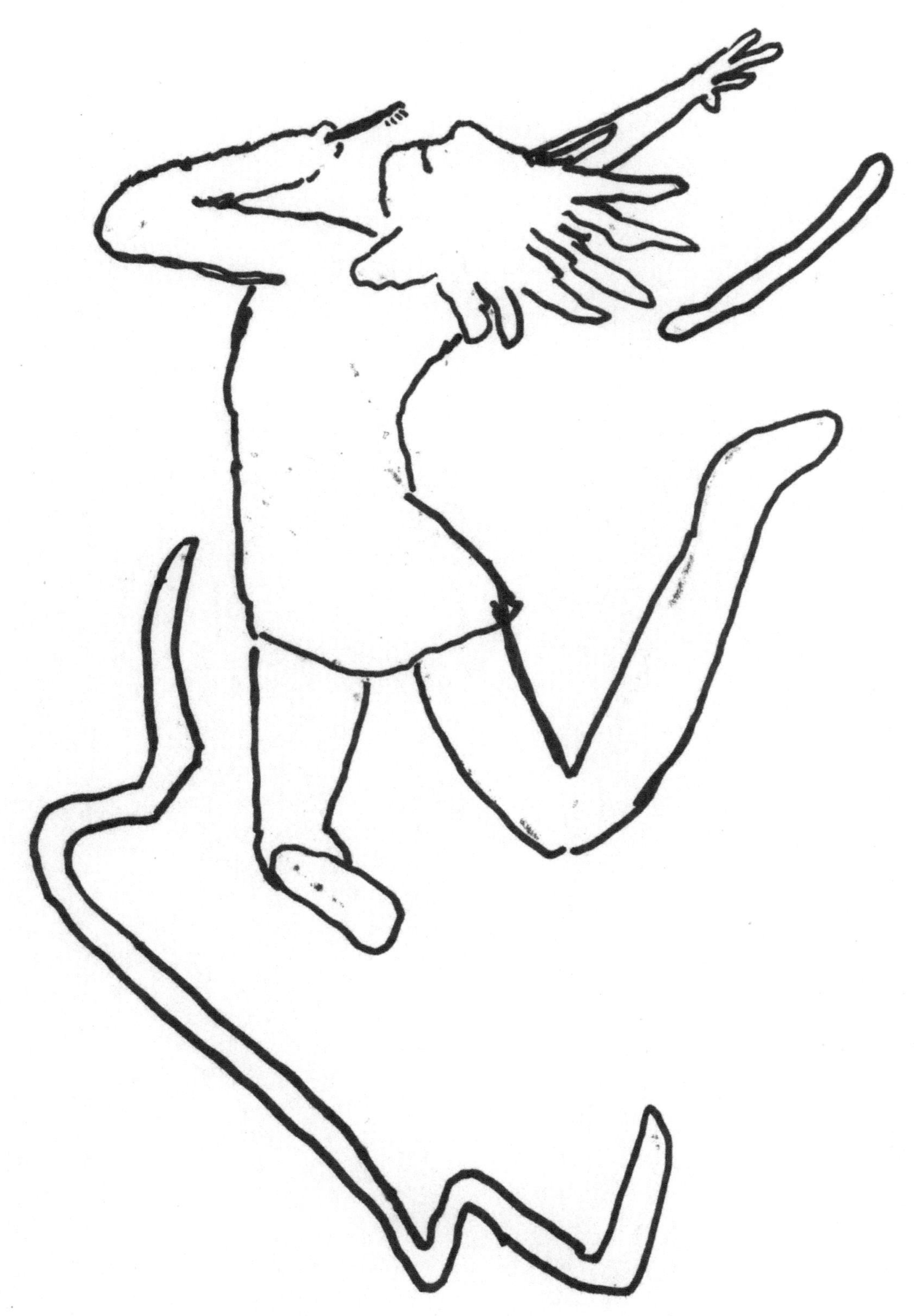

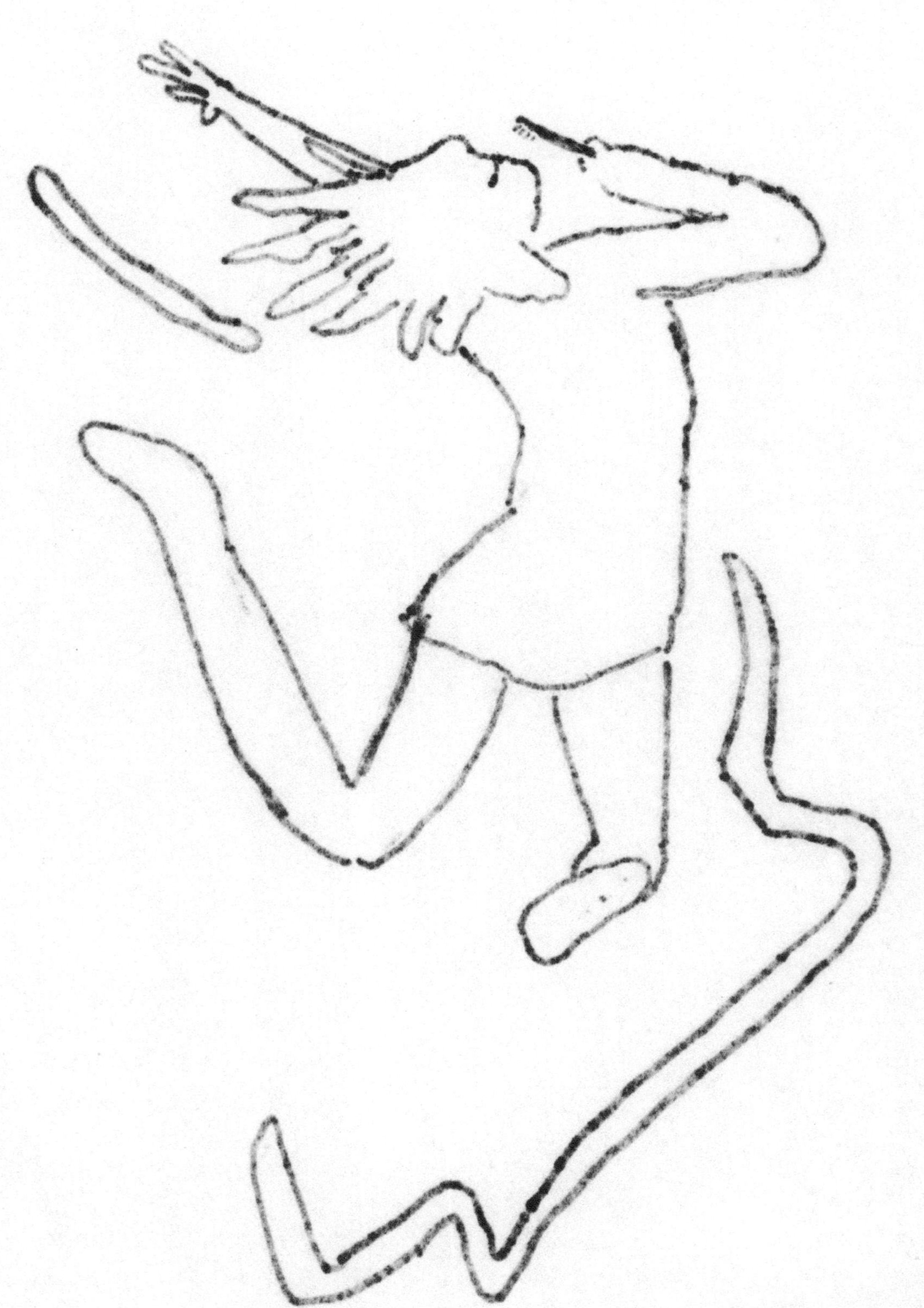

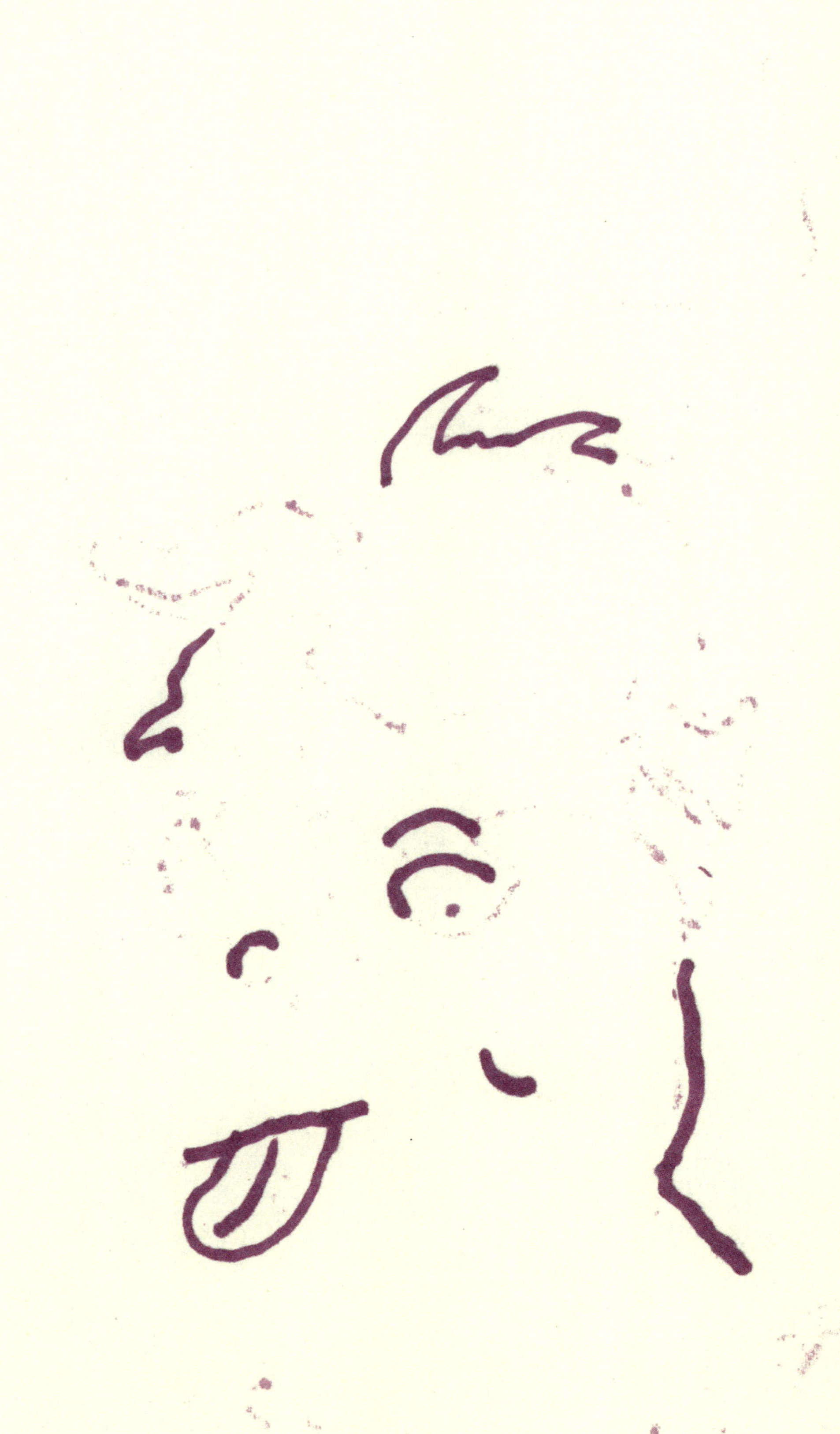

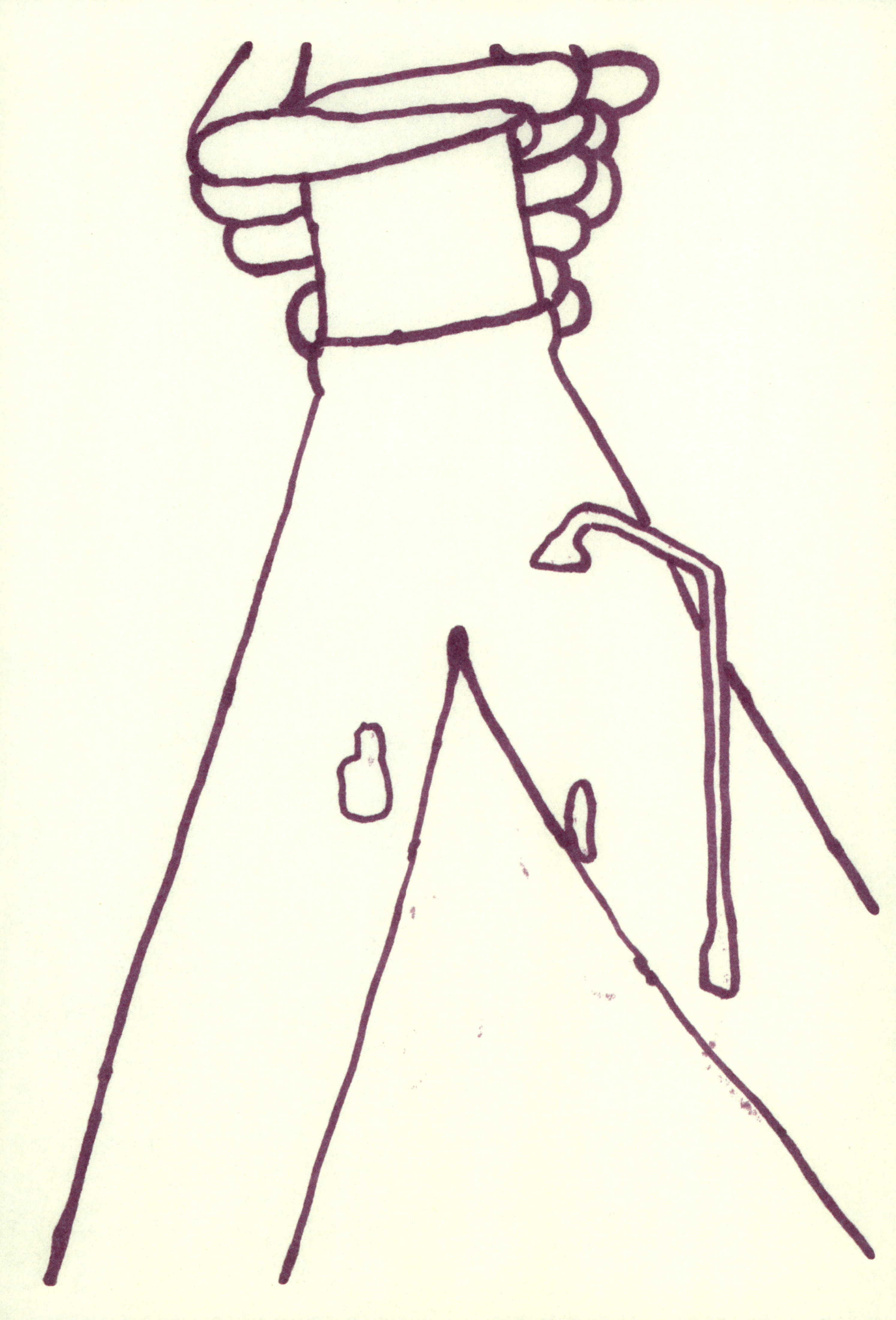

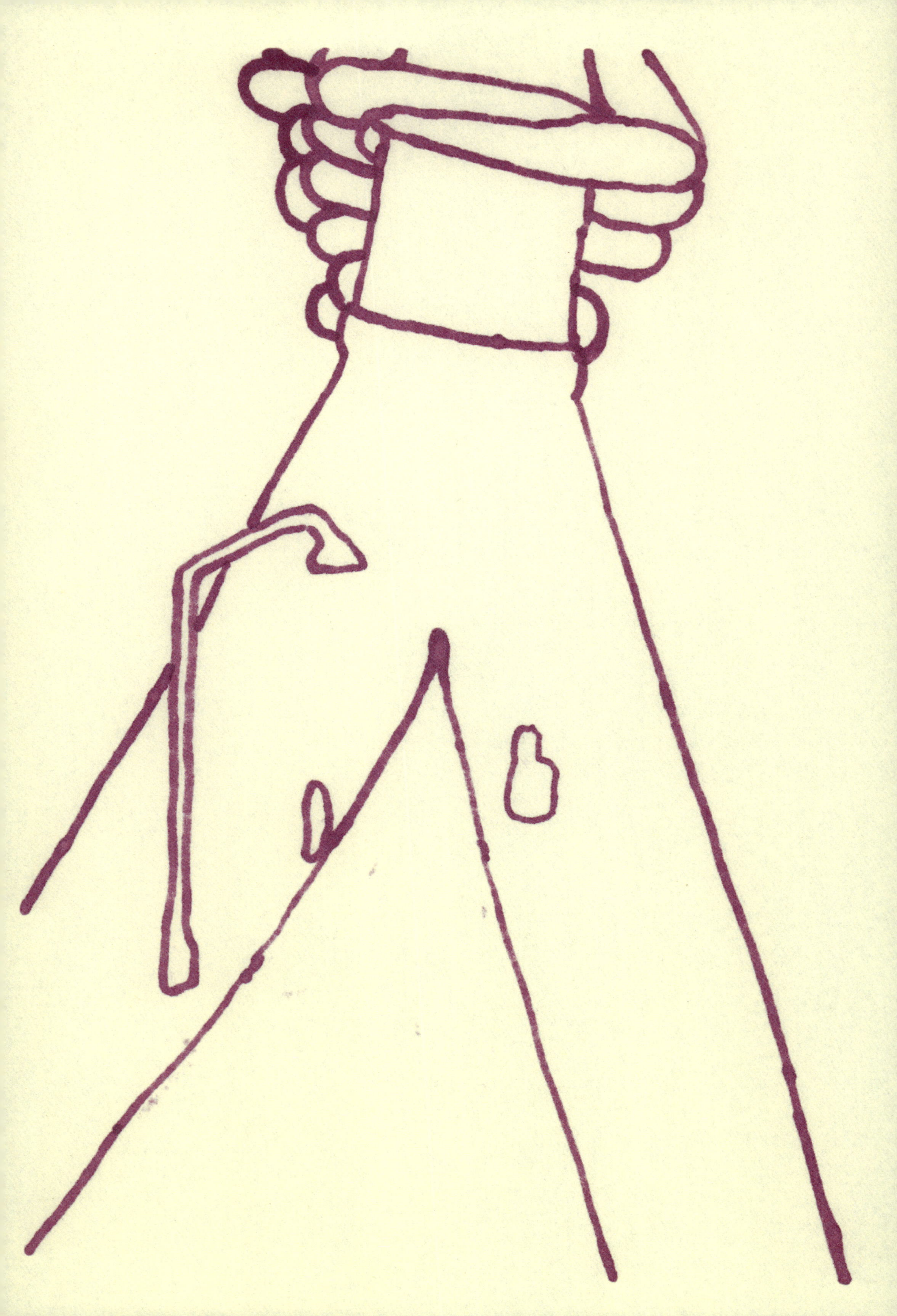

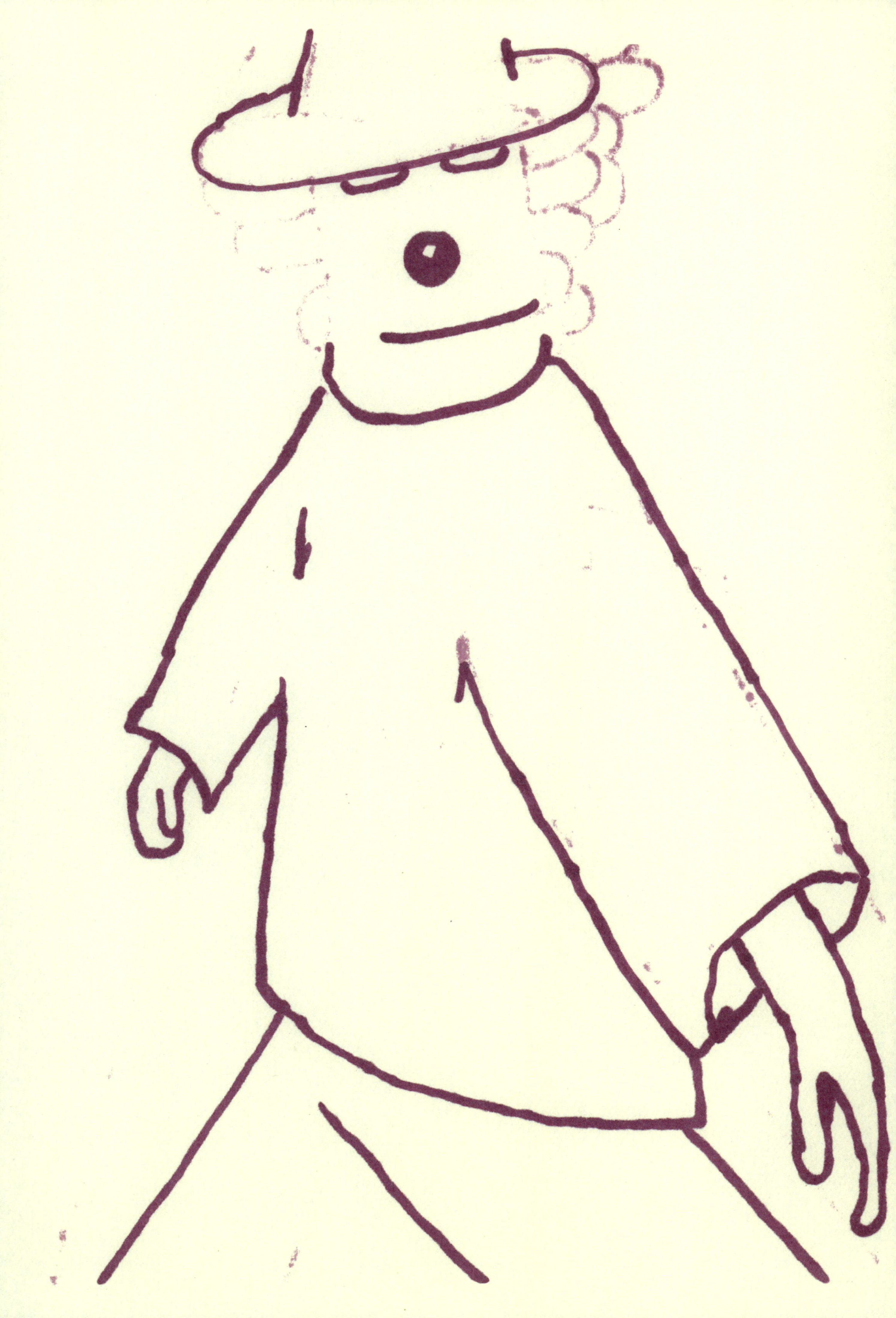

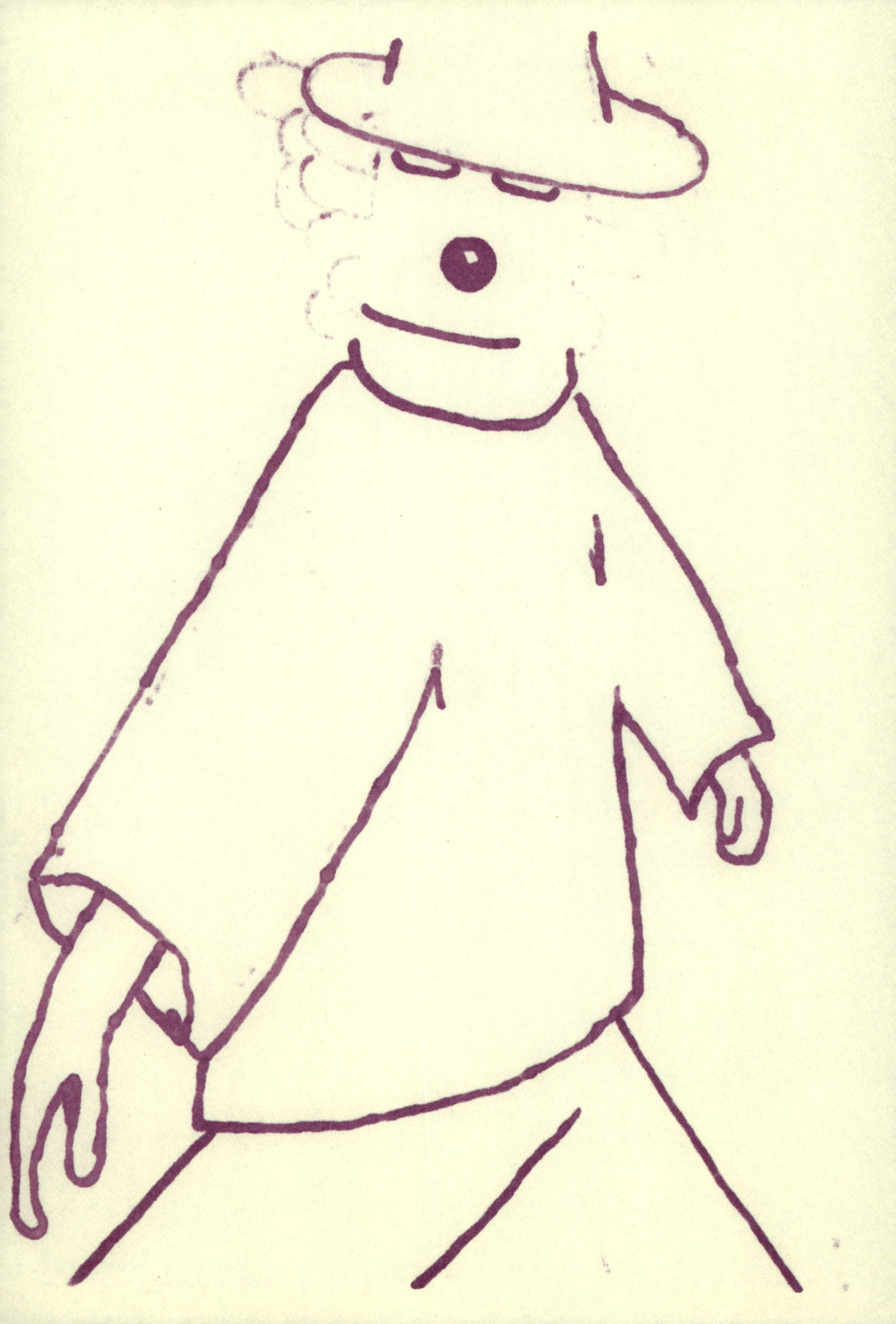

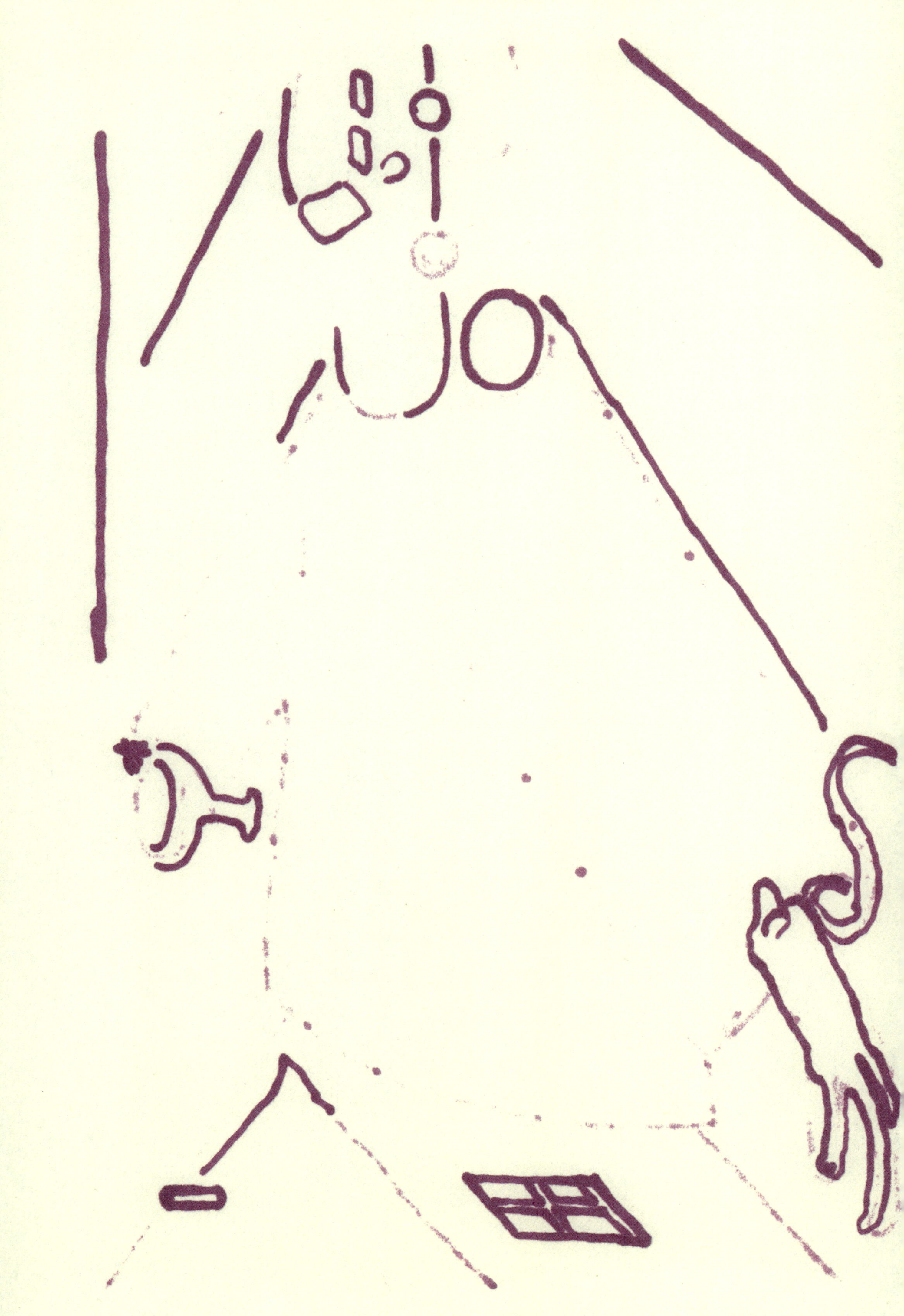

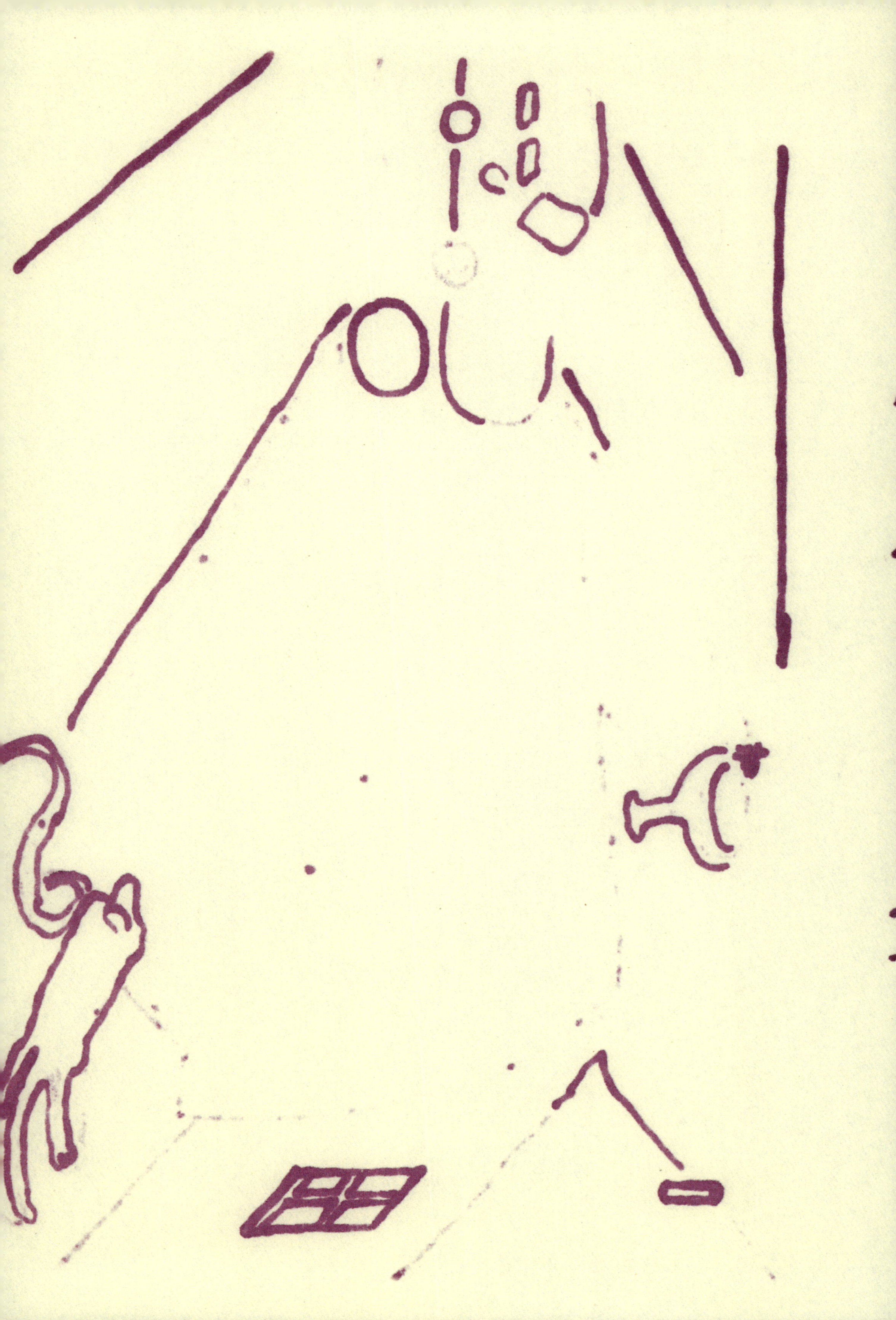

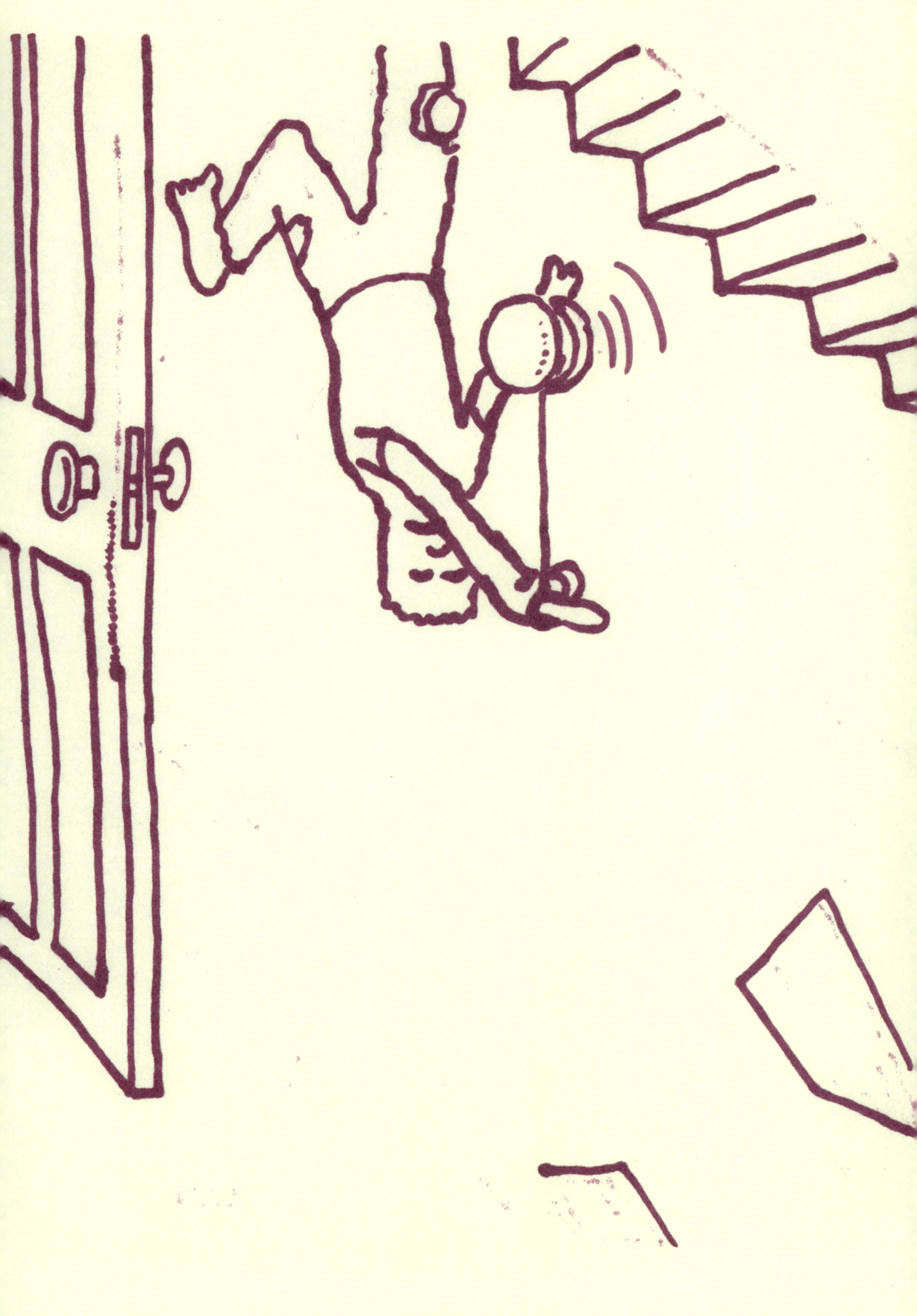

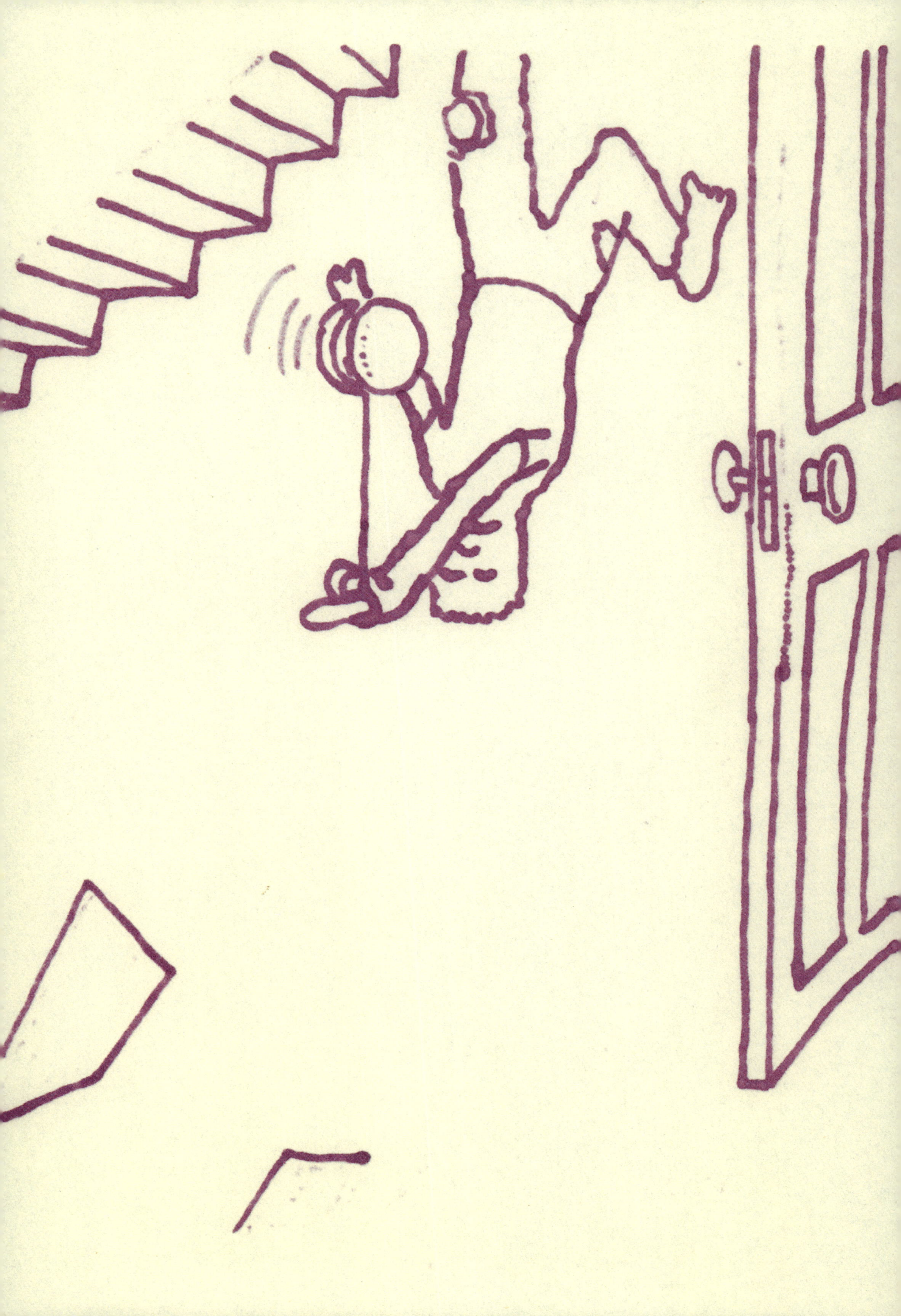

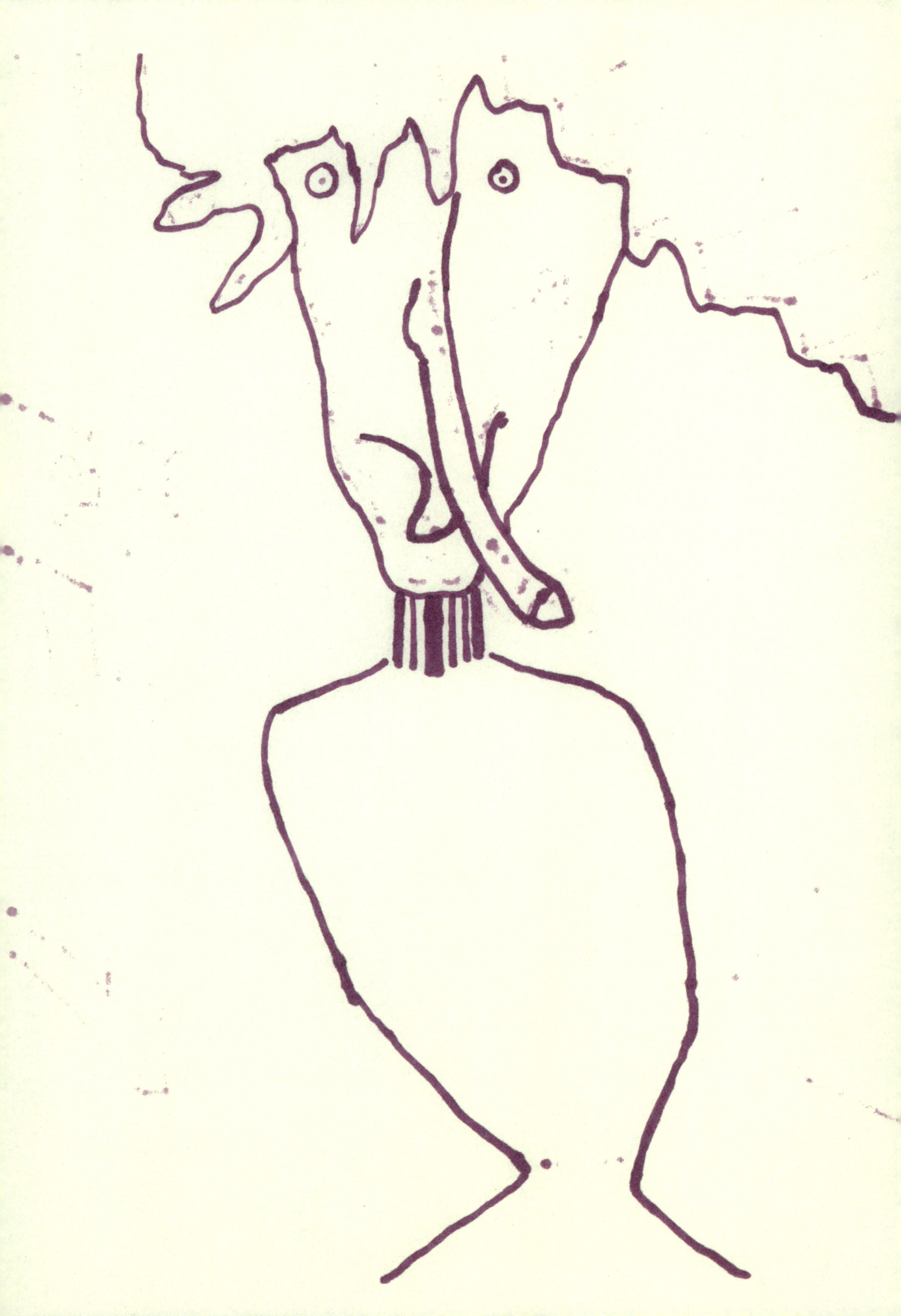

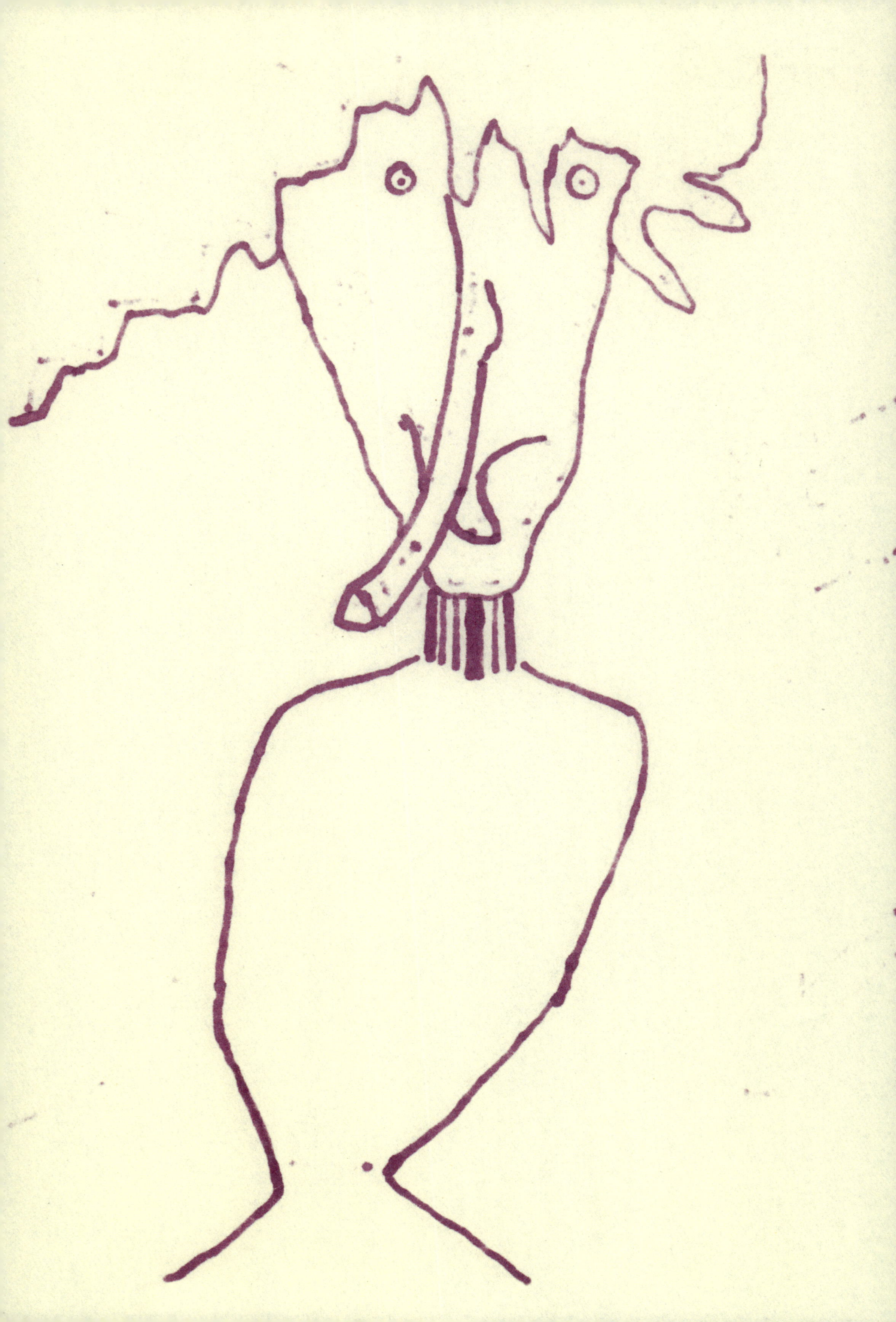

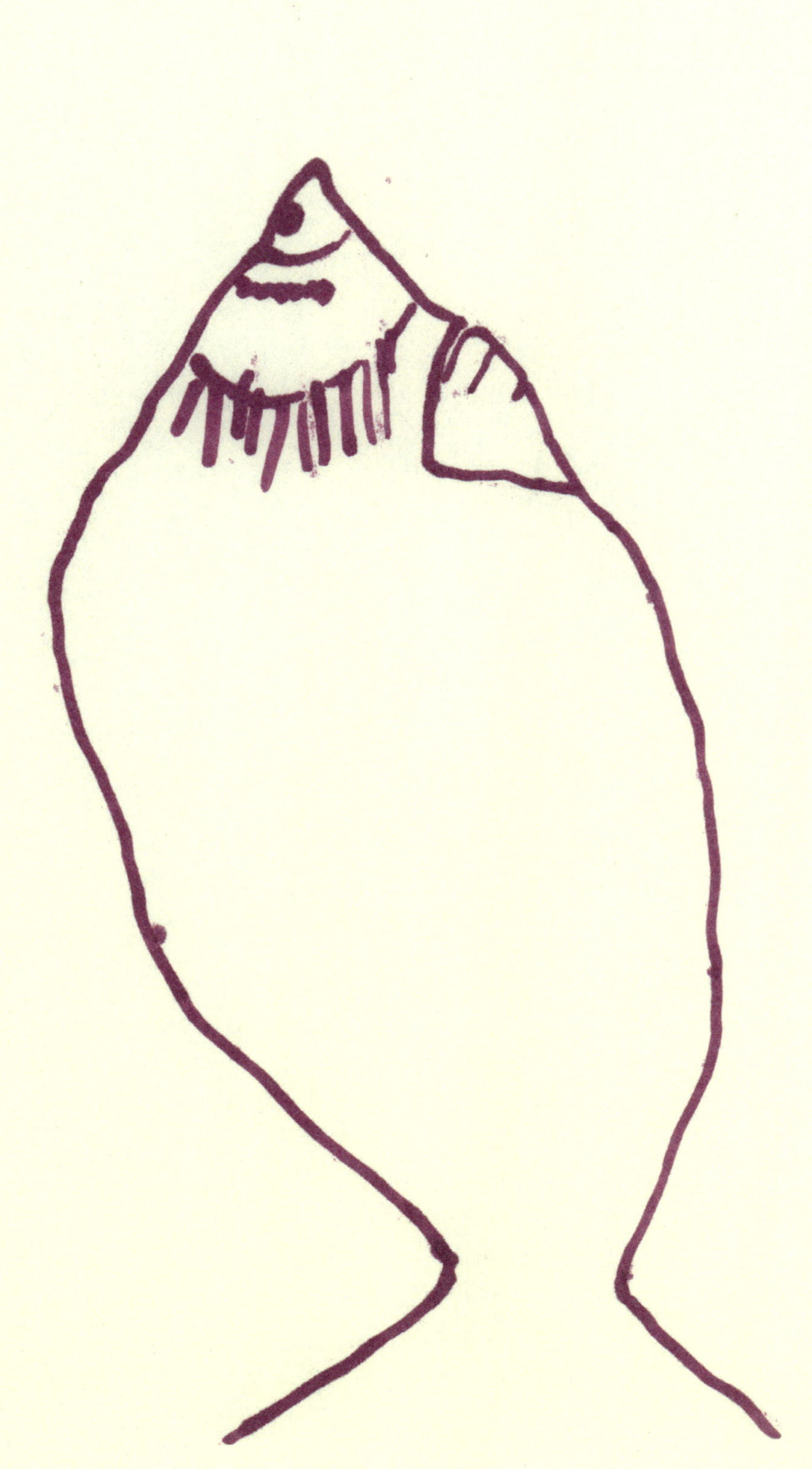

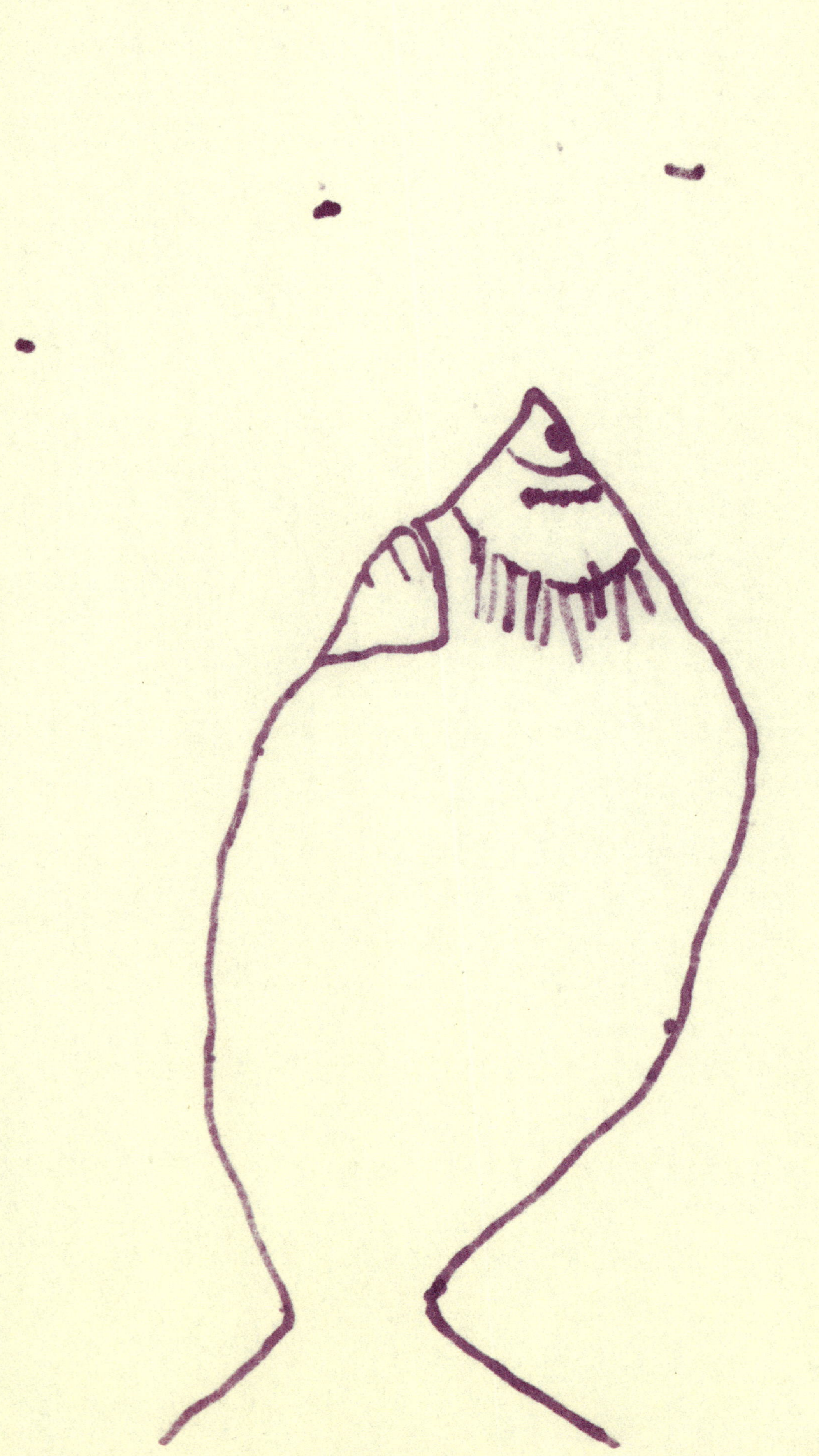

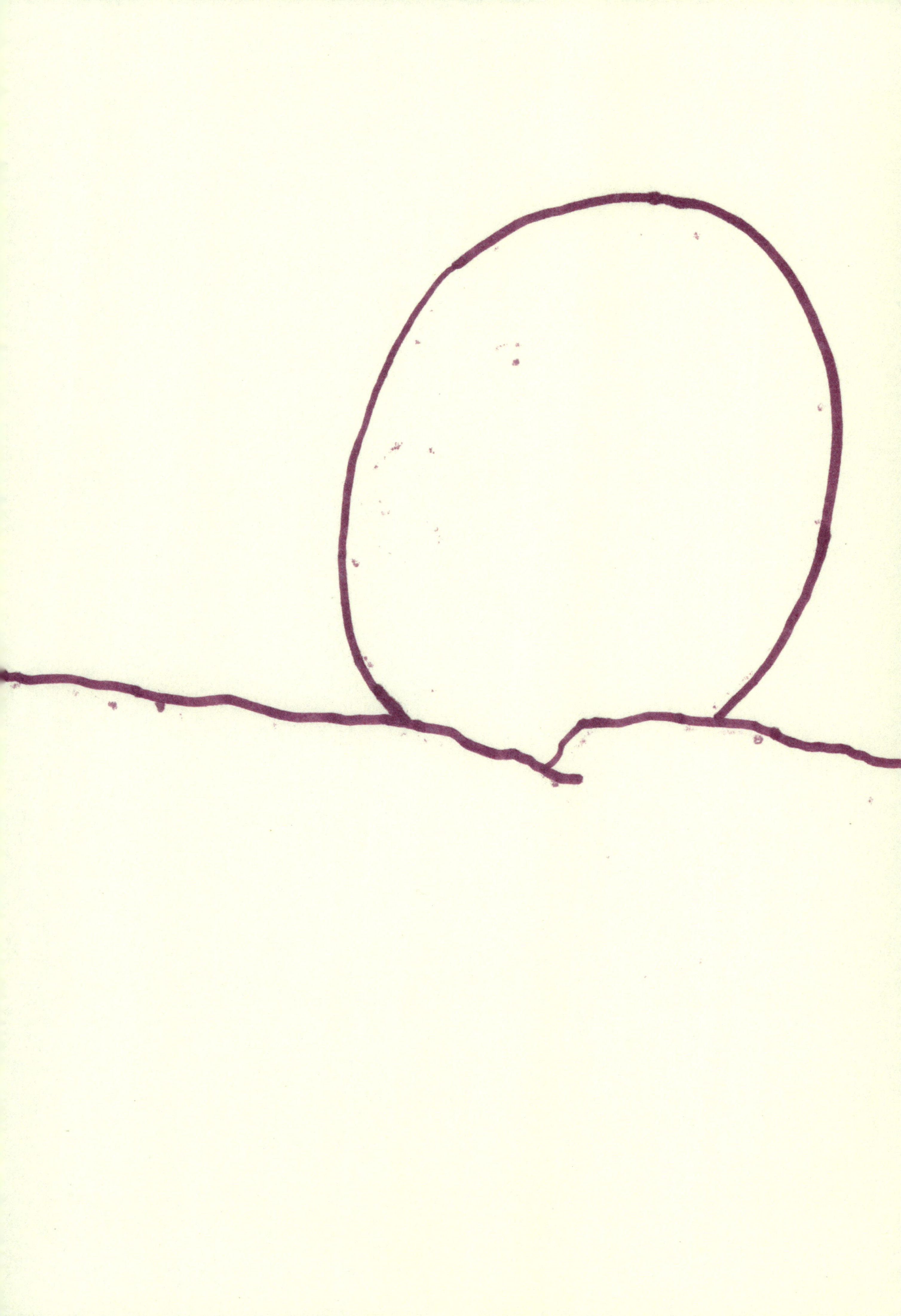

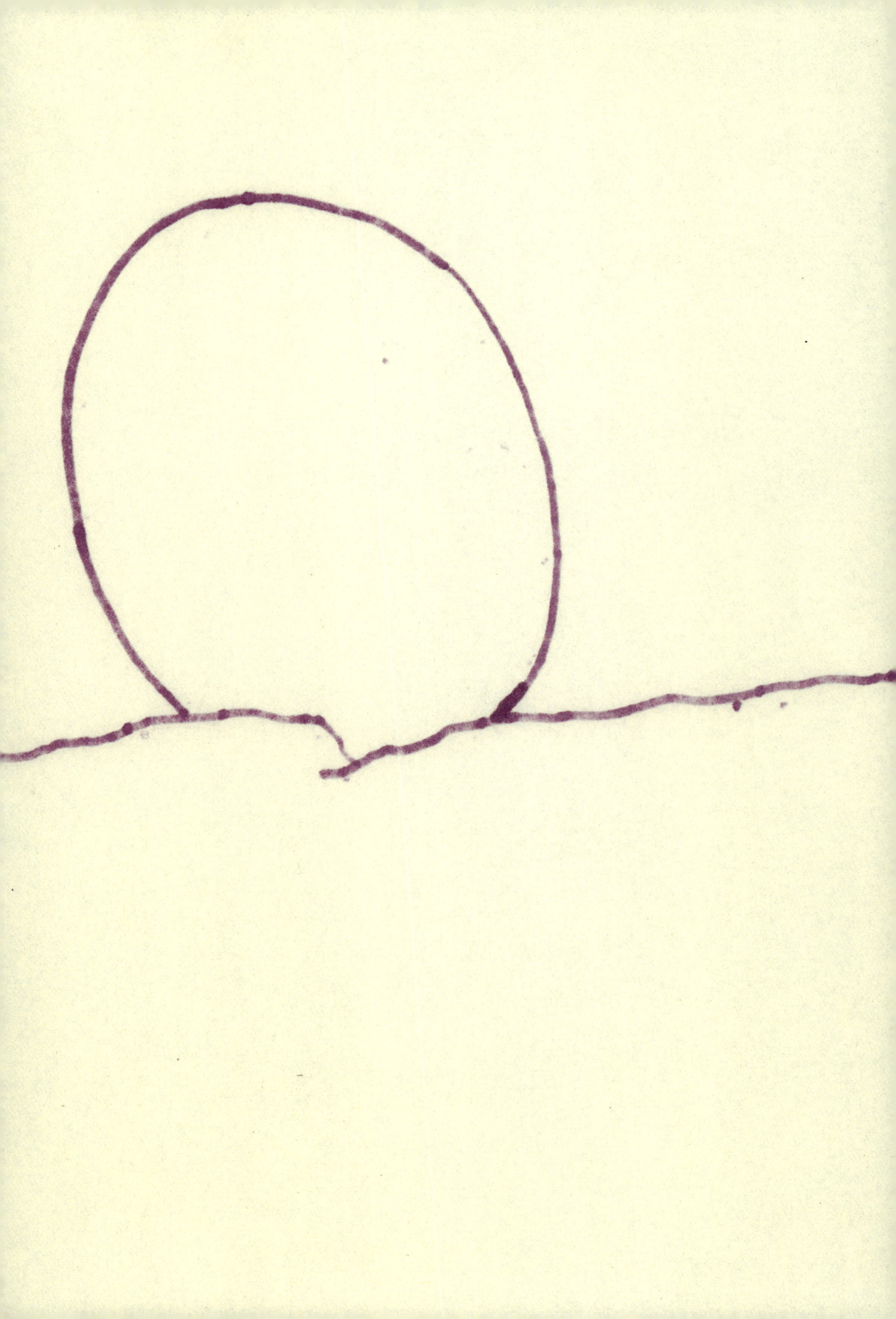

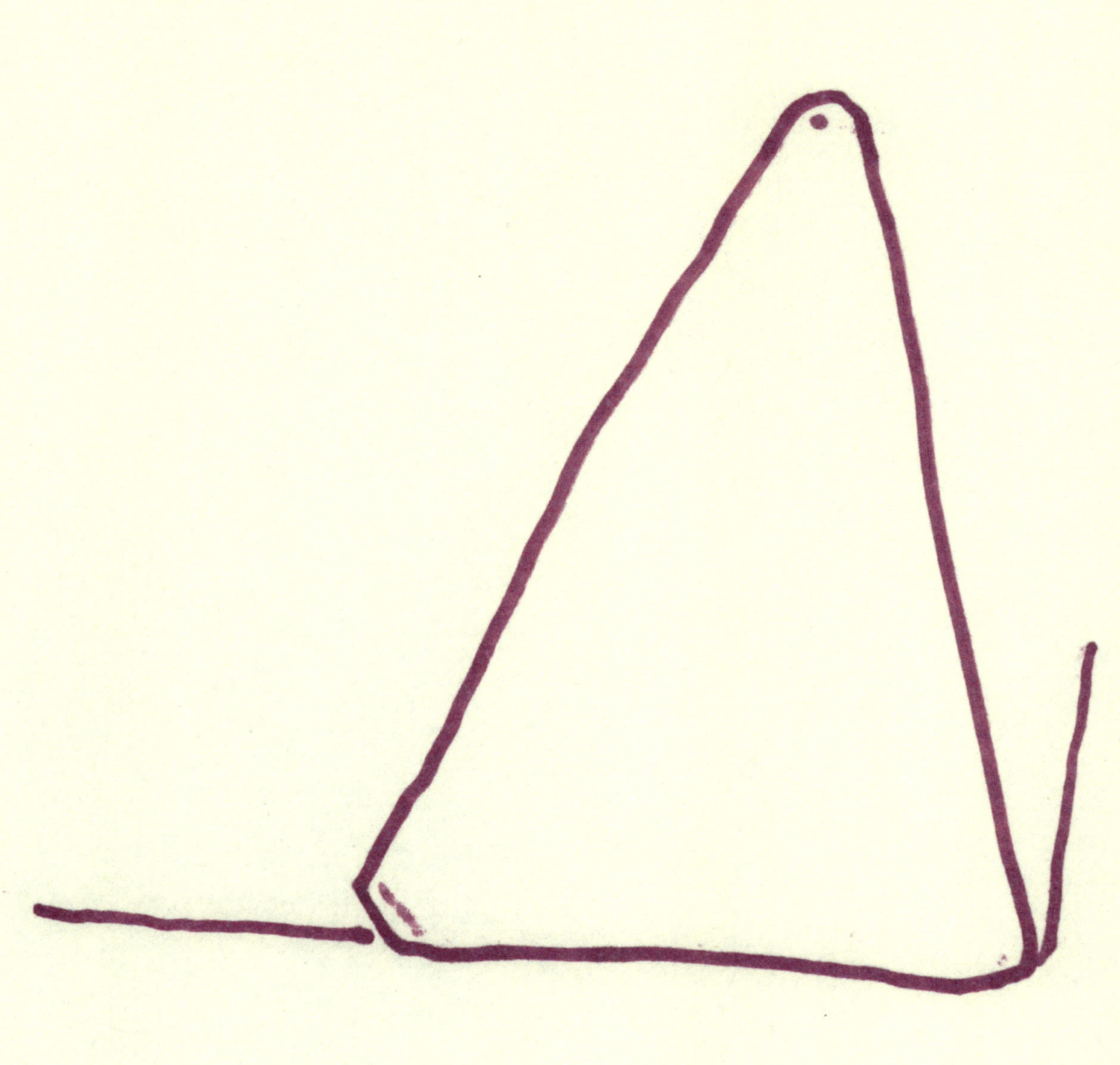

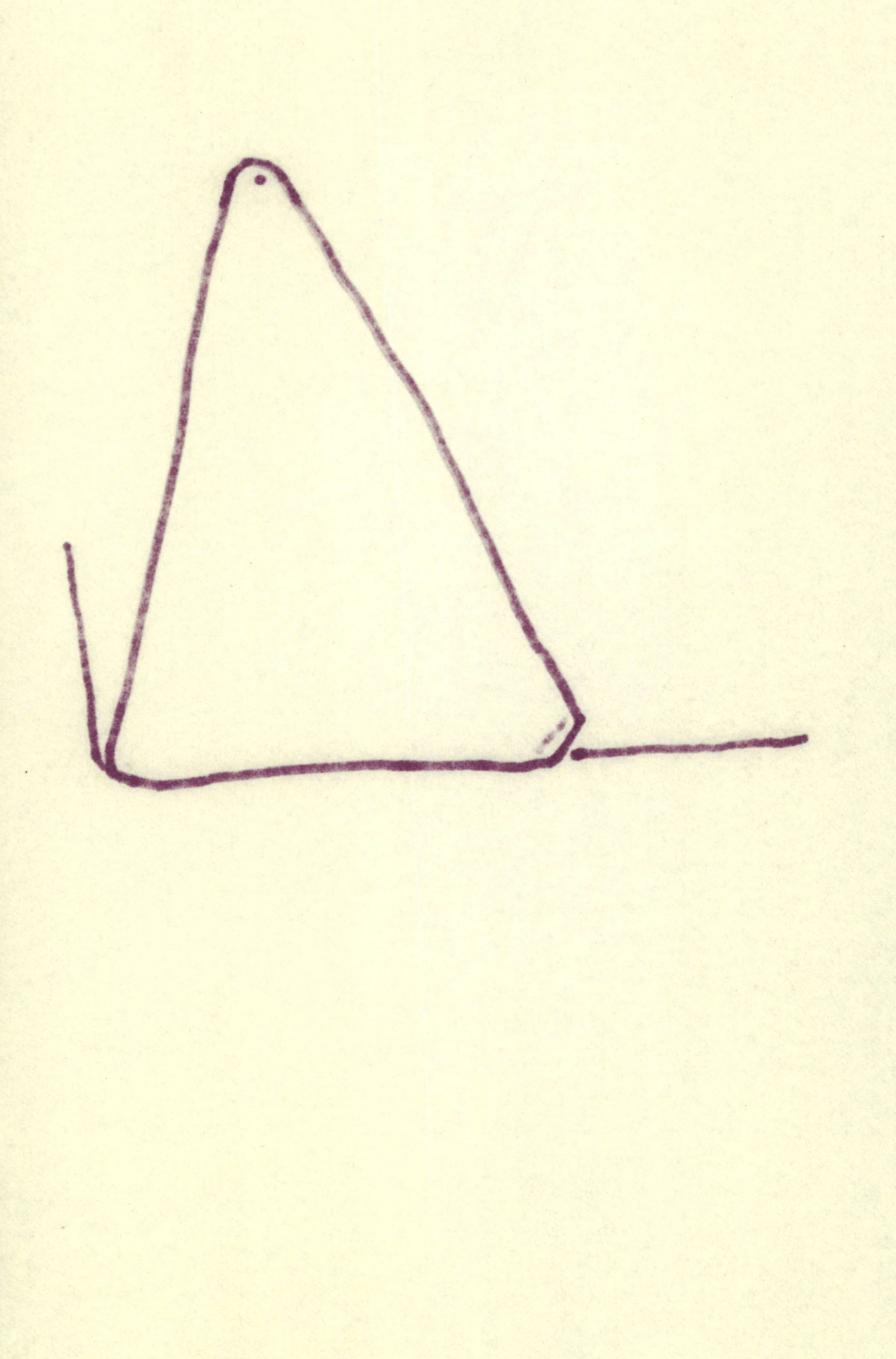

Michael Williams
Things You Shouldn't
Understand

Published by
Karma, New York

Edition of 750

ISBN 978-1-942607-63-2